TAKING CHILDREN SERIOUSLY

TAKING CHILDREN SERIOUSLY

Proven Strategies for Building Self-Esteem

Margaret F. Skutch
with
Sherry Andrews

WORD BOOKS
PUBLISHER
WACO, TEXAS

A DIVISION OF
WORD, INCORPORATED

Library of Congress Cataloging-in-Publication Data

Skutch, Margaret F. , 1932–
    Taking children seriously : proven strategies for building self-
esteem / Margaret F. Skutch with Sherry Andrews.
        p.   cm.
    Bibliography : p.
    ISBN 0-8499-0652-0
    1. Self-respect in children.   2. Learning ability.   I. Andrews,
Sherry, 1953–   . II. Title.
BF723.S3S58   1988
649'.1—dc19   88-18081
                                                                CIP
Printed in the United States of America
8 9 8 0 1 2 3 9   RRD   9 8 7 6 5 4 3 2 1

Acknowledgments

I would like to dedicate this book to my sons, David and Christopher, who taught me how to take children seriously. I also here acknowledge the help of Mary Jo Townsend, Joanne Brooks, and Norma Bryan, who encouraged me—with lots of handholding and more practical help, such as cooking—to write the thesis on which this book is based. And finally, my thanks goes to Will Hamlin, my collaborator on *To Start a School*, whose shadow is felt on many of these pages.

Contents

Preface

In 1962, I began to look for a nursery school for my son David. The results of my search were disappointing. The pink and blue schools I saw were dirty, noisy places lacking peace and joy. The teachers put the children down by the way they spoke to them and the rough way they touched them. Even the furniture seemed to be selected without consideration for the children who used it. The early childhood programs available did not offer the respect and quality I felt all children deserved.

My heartsick feelings about these places prompted me to do research at Yale where I met Dr. Omar Khayyam Moore. Dr. Moore, who developed the "talking typewriter" for his daughter and for children all over the world, suggested that Montessori would be a valuable starting point for further research. I was delighted to "discover" Maria Montessori. Her philosophy sparked my enthusiasm and led me to enroll in a graduate program at Fairleigh Dickinson University, which introduced me to Piaget and the concepts of "new math" as well as giving me an official diploma from The American Montessori Society.

The fall of 1963 saw David and I enrolled at Whitby School in Greenwich, Connecticut, the first Montessori in the country—David as a student and I as an intern teacher. And in 1964, I started the Montessori School of Stamford, Connecticut, in a church building. Two years later, the school was moved to its current location into a building I helped design specifically for the purpose of conveying the Montessori principles of learning. Although Montessori's techniques were still predominant, I began to stretch her exercises and to develop new teaching tools. The school was renamed the Early Learning Center and my personal journey as an educator truly began.

During the twenty years since the school's inception, new ideas were tried and tested, continually. I matured as an educator through this process. I learned to trust my own ideas based on firsthand observation of the children and to listen to the ideas of others who were involved. The school and the strategies I developed there earned grants from such groups as the Educational Facilities Laboratories of the Ford Foundation, and The Connecticut Commission on the Arts. I was named as consultant to the U.S. Office of Education and the Far West Laboratories for Educational Research and Development, and later became the educational director, facility designer, and staff trainer for the C. & P. Telephone Company Day Care Center in Washington, D.C.

As I became recognized as an innovator in early childhood education, the Early Learning Center also received recognition as a teacher training institute—the Early Learning Center Institute. There, teachers and parents observed and learned methods of classroom design and management as well as a philosophy that builds a child's self-esteem and the adult's trust of children. Original materials from the Early Learning Center and Montessori were shared so that they could be replicated back home.

Preface

The Early Learning Center has its own story. The present building, erected in 1967 at 12 Gary Road, in Stamford, is a low, white structure tucked into a rolling meadow and flanked by evergreens. Boulders that were dug up from the building site are placed around the yard, and a giant mulberry bush as tall as the school blooms every spring. Maples and apple trees dot the grounds and truck loads of sand were brought in to form a sand area. A trampoline was built into a pit dug by the parents and a lobster boat heels over slightly in the schoolyard. The school is surrounded by a rail fence closing in the one acre that belongs to the nonprofit controlling organization.

Of course, the story of the school doesn't begin with this building, but the building represents several milestones for me. The first is the commitment of the parents and the staff to further the efforts of early childhood learning. The second is the extension of our teaching philosophy into the physical environment. At long last, it seemed to me (although three years is a remarkably short time in which to start a school and build a building), we had a building that supported our purpose.

Initially, however, the school was located at a church. The staff of The Montessori School of Stamford was compelled to work diligently each morning to recreate the exciting environment for learning, since all the school's effects had to be packed away each day after school. This was a phase of growth and transition since it was during this time that the school evolved from its more rigid Montessori origin to the more flexible Early Learning Center.

A unique aspect of the school was the involvement of the parents of the children in the education process. Because of the role structure and the recordkeeping techniques which are described in this book, parents, regardless of their educational background, could take an

11

active role in their children's education. We believed that the function of the teacher was to guide children to learn from themselves rather than to didactically impart information appropriate for a child of two or three. This belief allowed the school to move into the next stage of its development: that of a teacher-training institute.

A teacher at the Early Learning Center was someone who felt a genuine love for children and a desire to teach them. A teacher could be a parent, a high-school student, or a state-certified teacher; it didn't matter. Every teacher shared in every phase of teaching the children. No position was restricted to the novice, because the recordkeeping system provided the framework for every teacher to follow. The daily coaching session guaranteed that even the most "green" of teachers quickly became a seasoned professional. What was recognized above all other credentials was an individual's concern for the children. Even the director of the school rotated roles and on any given day might assume the role of Rover, Greeter, or Head Teacher. There was no hierarchy of the teaching staff.

To gain a better understanding of the school as a teacher-training institute, it is necessary to see the whole picture. Beyond the line of evergreen trees on the adjacent two acres of land, I bought an old home, circa 1799. The home was a delight, the walk to school invigorating and restorative each morning and evening. Not only was it my home but it also provided lodging for the teachers of the school who often stayed one or two years in their residency. Each afternoon the staff would review its daily work in the coaching session at the school, and each evening we would enjoy lively conversations on education over dinner in the relaxed and peaceful environment of my dining room. This was truly a resident apprenticeship for the teachers and myself.

During the past twenty years at the Early Learning Center, the methodologies were refined and the craft of teaching honed to a fine art of loving children and letting them learn. In its current phase, a protégé of mine, Maureen Murphy, has taken on the directorship of the school so that it is getting to be better and better. The school is now renamed the Children's Learning Center. And although the teachers no longer reside in the home near the school, there is still a concerted effort to preserve the close association of the staff.

The ideals of early childhood learning that we worked to establish will continue to be pursued at the Children's Learning Center. There is a substantial waiting list for entrance to the school, which indicates to me that a growing number of parents are concerned with their preschoolers' development. The school will continue to evolve with the needs of its children, but the underlying respect and trust for the children will always guide its development.

The attention that the school and I received prompted me to share my experience in my first book, *To Start a School,* published in 1971. Since writing *To Start a School* with Wilfrid G. Hamlin, I have continued to study how young children learn. That first book was written to tell of the experience of starting a school. This book is written to share five strategies for building the self-esteem of children which I developed during my tenure at the Early Learning Center. I see this as the vital element essential to the learning process.

The ideas presented in *Taking Children Seriously* can be easily used by teachers and parents. They require only a heartfelt commitment to the child and his or her development. It is my wish that what I have written, with Sherry Andrews' help, will inspire you and guide you in treating children with the courtesy and respect they deserve.

Part I

LOVING CHILDREN AND LETTING THEM LEARN

1

Taking Children Seriously

Many great thinkers have turned their attention to the subject of building a man's (or woman's) self-esteem. What I've done is apply some of the best of their thoughts to the process of early childhood learning. The operative words here are *early* and *learning*. It is not, nor has it ever been, my intention to turn out young soldiers who can recite, read, count, and do math solely to enable their parents to say, "Johnny is only three years old and can already read, write, add, and subtract." I don't want to be in the assembly-line production business.

In fact, I do not produce anything. What I do is aid

children in discovering their own innate problem-solving abilities. I also help them make sense of all that surrounds them by presenting them with options for learning and by using the vast array of learning materials available. There is direction to their learning. Each child's learning for each day follows what the child is ready to learn, as well as the individual goals I have set for him.

John Holt, a respected educator with whom I occasionally agree, expressed this educational philosophy in one sentence: "What they [children] need from us is not orders and usually not even much advice or help, but access to the world—to places and experiences . . . , to people . . . , and to tools and resources, including books, music, and the raw materials of art and science."

Of course, Holt was not the first to express these feelings. In the sixteenth century, Montaigne said, "The authority of those who teach is often an obstacle to those who want to learn."

I first discovered just how many obstacles to learning we place in children's way when I began looking for a nursery school in Stamford, Connecticut, for my son David in 1962. A thirty-year-old housewife with one two-and-a-half-year-old child and another on the way, I had little thought of becoming a teacher and certainly even less of starting a school when I set out on that fateful fall morning. I simply hoped to find a school that would encourage David's natural curiosity and provide him with a variety of opportunities for learning. But, as I visited the various nursery schools in Stamford it quickly became apparent that the opposite was happening. Children were placed in such structured, inhibiting situations or in environments with so little stimulation that their innate desire to learn was stifled.

In *To Start a School*, that Will Hamlin and I wrote in 1971, we described some of those schools. There was the pink and blue nursery with frilly white curtains that presented the child's world as "sweet, cute, full of pastel colors and baby animals as portrayed in cheap children's books." Such a babyland-fantasy environment promised no learning about the real world.

A parents' cooperative school that I visited was real enough—but not in any positive sense. There, "a dozen children were pulling each other's hair while three mothers gossiped over coffee in the kitchen and a sixteen-year-old high-school dropout tried to maintain order."

I was equally unimpressed by the academy-type school, where a highly structured program kept the tiny children moving on command from one activity to another. It fostered imitation, not what I would consider true learning. The tiny children sat in rows and were drilled in vocabulary. After a ten-minute recess, they began their art lesson for the day, stringing beads—ten white ones, then a blue one, then more white ones, then a red one.

A fourth type, the play school, offered freedom for creative play with its multitude of ragged toys, battered blocks, tricycles, and dolls, but heaven forbid any child should want to learn to read. The school believed that childhood was too brief and precious a time to be spoiled by having children learn letters or numbers.

When Will and I wrote about these schools, I thought they would be history in just a few years. Such marvelous things were being discovered in preschool education. Furthermore, at the Early Learning Center (ELC), we were actually proving that there were far more effective ways to help children learn—methods that eliminated the stress for both children and teachers which existed in most nursery schools. The publicity we received and the enthusiasm of the numerous educators who visited ELC convinced me that our methods were having an influence. I was still very naive about the educational system. I thought that once better teaching methods were developed, they would be quickly adopted. After all, in science or medicine as

19

soon as some helpful discovery is made it is put into practice. As soon as we learned how to send a man to the moon we sent him. We have known better ways of teaching for years and yet we still face a crisis in education. Isn't it sad that where the lives of our children are concerned we are so slow to implement improvements?

I have visited many nursery schools in recent years, so I have witnessed how little improvement has taken place. There have been some superficial changes—furniture and facilities have been scaled down to child-size—but they are still chaotic, noisy places lacking peace and joy. In these "sand and sunshine" schools, as I call them, children learn sing-a-long songs, take naps, eat little snacks, and are admonished to "share" supplies. They learn to survive. Parents seem to like this model because it allows children to play just as if they were at home (assuaging parents' guilt for having to work and leave the child) without forcing the child to learn too much.

A variation on this model is the new corporate-style kindergarten. Franchised like hamburger chains, these centers have replaced the noise and dirt of traditional nursery schools with a sterile, almost antiseptic environment. Designed to conform to a model and run on a cost-effective basis, they seem more like factories turning out what has been facetiously called "Kentucky-fried children" than centers where children are encouraged to develop their own unique talents and abilities.

Although they teach children to recite their ABC's and to count, I question how much genuine learning occurs in most of these centers. A school that I observed recently was typical in its highly structured approach to instruction. I saw six to eight children corraled into a math center where the teacher directed everyone to watch her lay down three plastic cubes. She proceeded to drill and question them and only when she gave permission could a child pick up the cubes and lay down three himself. The teacher was satisfied when each, by rote memory, could feed back to her the word *three* when she held up three fingers. Those children were not gaining any true understanding of mathematical concepts; they were simply parroting back a memorized response.

The effects of this "standardization" of child care are most evident in art activities. Art is an area that perhaps gives a child the best opportunity to be creative and daring and free because there is no need for limiting directions, except in caring for the materials and cleaning up. Yet at one school I watched a teacher pass out precut cardboard hearts, since Valentine's Day was approaching. She then gave the children red paint and brushes to paint their hearts, and that was their art experience for the day!

In another school classroom, I saw rows of boats with halves of paper plates as hulls and lollipop sticks as masts. A single crayon had been used to color each hull. Other examples of what I call "copycat" art lined the remaining walls or hung from the ceiling. The visual effect of the hundreds of colored papers disturbed me as much as the lack of creativity. The room looked and felt chaotic.

The play-yards of many of these schools are as structured as the classrooms. They are usually small areas which rarely have grass. Sometimes, the ground is actually covered with wood chips so there remains almost nothing of God's creation for the children to enjoy. Often a slide, a few swings, and a set of monkey bars for climbing are the only equipment. And, with all the teachers outside strictly supervising, spontaneous play is discouraged.

One day on one of these playgrounds, I noticed a three-year-old boy eyeing my coat. It was tweed in a lush textured fabric, and I could tell from his gaze that he wanted to touch it. Taking a cue from my smile, he walked toward me. Immediately the teacher screamed, "Get back in line, Johnny!" and the child, humiliated that he had dared follow his urge, quickly melted back into the line—no longer an individual. He was learning early to suppress his desire to explore and to limit his interests to what the teacher allowed.

Another day, the director of a child-care center pointed to a small play area enclosed by a chain link fence and said proudly, "Here are our two-year-olds." I stooped down, poking through the fence to talk to these children and suddenly I felt like I was at the pound, looking at the puppies in their cages. I had a sudden desire to open the gate and shout, "Run, kids, run! Don't ever come back!" Instead, I got in my car and wept. I wondered whether the parents of those children realized how controlled and barren that environment was. Were they comfortable leaving their children there or did they simply have no choice? Perhaps they were not even aware of how much their children could benefit from a freer, more stimulating environment.

Another school that remains popular is the academic nursery. Nurtured on the anxieties of upper-middle-class parents who want to insure that their children get a head start on being admitted to a prestigious university, these schools have flourished in recent years. With their emphasis on academic excellence, these schools mold little minds through rigid discipline, purposing to produce little soldiers—especially "smart" soldiers. The walls of the school are lined, not with drawings as in a nursery school, but with samples of each child's lessons. Reading, writing, and arithmetic have become buzz words for parents to trot out for friends and family as they prompt their child to demonstrate what he or she has learned. Foreign languages add to the prestige of the school and emphasize its intent as a place for serious learning. With their rigid schedules and the unrelenting pressure they place on children, they remind me of the infamous Japanese "cram schools."

A Serious Danger

What concerns me about all of these schools is the way they stifle creativity. I think we are in serious danger of producing a generation of adults who cannot think for themselves. I say that, first, because preschoolers at ages two-and-a-half to six are in the crucial formative years of development and, second, because most of the nursery school child-care centers that I see provide a rigid, authoritarian environment that discourages individual thinking. The situations still fit the description of schools decried by the famed Carnegie Corporation report in 1970. That study found that most schools are preoccupied with order, control, and routine for the sake of routine. They practice systematic repression of the students and promote docility, passivity, and conformity, which destroy student curiosity. More seriously, students' desires and abilities to think for themselves are suppressed.

The lack of change in our schools would be less distressing if our society had remained relatively static. But we have experienced a tremendous cultural shift during the past twenty-five years, which has made the need for better quality early childhood education even more critical.

In the wave of nostalgia that seems to be washing over the country today, we hear a lot about restoring "traditional family values"—the kind of values portrayed in TV programs like "Father Knows Best," "Ozzie and Harriet," and "Leave It to Beaver."

A character on the popular show "Designing Women" recently seemed to express both the dilemmas of life in the eighties and our desire to return to a simpler time. A divorced mother of two, trying to juggle Christmas schedules with her ex-husband, her current boyfriend (who also had children), and his ex-wife, she sighed, "I'd give anything for a good, old-fashioned Ward Cleaver Christmas." So would a lot of us, I suspect. I also suspect that those perfect TV families were mostly fantasy. But they did portray family life accurately in one important respect: For the most part, nuclear families stayed intact then and few mothers worked. If this was stifling to many women, as they later claimed, it generally provided a stable environment for children.

When I started my school, I sometimes had trouble convincing mothers to allow their children to attend for even three hours in the morning. Today, children are dropped off at day centers at 6 A.M. and picked up at 6 P.M.

In 1963, only 19 percent of the mothers who had preschool children worked. Today, 60 percent work and more are flooding into the job market every year. In the next ten years, the number of children under six requiring daytime supervision is expected to grow by more than 50 percent! Professor Edward Zigler, professor of psychology at Yale and an authority on child care, notes: "It is scaring everybody that a whole generation of children is being raised in a way that has never happened before."

Dr. Urie Bronfenbrenner, distinguished family sociologist, author and founding architect of Operation Head Start, says that two of the greatest and most consequential changes in American life in recent years are working parents and single parents.

"Hecticness" in American life is a primary cause of the instability and chaos he sees as one trigger of alienation in families. Just the demands of transporting mother, father, and a child to and from their daily occupations is a strain, he says. He cites a Finnish study that followed a group of children from ages eight to thirty, showing that "instability" in a family is the strongest predictor of later antisocial behavior. By "instability" he means frequent changes in day-care arrangements or in parental employment, location, or schedule.

Fretting about the effects of day care on children has become a national preoccupation. No one knows what the effect will be on children to be reared by strangers. Studies from the "experts" only add to the confusion. Some, like Penn State's Belksky, suggest that extensive day care in the first year of life raises the risk of emotional problems. Others, like psychologist Margaret Burchinal, of the University of North Carolina, say that a mother's routine daily absence is not necessarily detrimental to her baby's emotional well-being.

Advantages of Quality Day Care

Studies of day care's effects on older children, especially those from deprived environments, are more definitive and more positive. In a study reported in the February 1987 issue of *Psychology Today,* Dr. Burchinal and her colleagues recruited 124 low-income children and randomly assigned some of them to research-based, high-quality day care. The others attended varying amounts of "good day care" (meeting federal guidelines) in the community. Using two standard tests of child development and a basic IQ test, the researchers compared the intellectual achievement of the children at various times through their fifty-fourth month. They discovered that those who attended the research day care outscored the community day-care group on average, but that both groups outscored those who attended little or no day care.

Another study, in Ypsilanti, Michigan, tracked the progress of preschool children who enrolled in quality day-care centers in 1962 until they graduated from high school. The study found that those who had attended day care were one half as likely to be on welfare, one half as likely to have a teen pregnancy, and twice as likely to have a job as those who did not attend day care. The study concluded that for every dollar invested in good day care, the state received five dollars.

25

Perhaps recognizing that it is in their best interest, by early 1988 several states had begun examining ways to insure that adequate day-care facilities are available for working mothers. The federal government has also joined the debate. With more than seventy bills before the U.S. Congress dealing with child care, as of Spring 1988, it seems inevitable that some form of child-care legislation will be enacted.

What concerns me most is the form of child care that will eventually predominate. We cannot afford to settle for simply providing more of the same basic types of child care that we have now. We are reminded daily that the United States is no longer the unchallenged leader of the world. Government and business leaders warn that we are in danger of losing our competitive edge in many areas—such as business, technology, science, or medicine. Americans need to be concerned that when we have the greatest need for creative, productive thinkers, there seems to be a growing deficiency in students' mental skills.

In the face of growing Japanese economic power, there has been much debate over the relative merits of the Japanese and American educational systems. I found it interesting that on a recent edition of "60 Minutes," a Japanese university professor criticized his country's system of rote learning for stifling creativity and innovative thinking. He pointed out that the United States has won twenty-three of the last thirty Nobel Prizes in Science while Japan has received one. If we are to have any hope of maintaining our leadership in the world, we must continue to produce those kinds of problem-solving people.

That will only happen if we begin helping our children to develop confidence in their thinking and problem-solving abilities at an early age. We must realize that the opinion a child forms about himself and his general approach to learning is generally fixed by the time he reaches first grade. People have to be able to take a risk in childhood to be able to take a risk when they grow up, to be problem solvers and thinkers. That's why I am so chagrined at the lack of thinking development that I see at so many child-care centers.

The good news is that it doesn't have to be that way. People have the tools to enable children to feel good about themselves, to take risks, to develop their ability to see answers, and to figure things out. We have used them with hundreds of children for almost twenty years at the Children's Learning Center and have proved that they work. I presented some of these techniques in *To Start a School*. In this book I will share five additional strategies for building self-esteem—communication, environment, roles, recordkeeping, and coaching—that we developed after *To Start a School* was published.

Although this book is directed primarily at educators, I want to emphasize that now, more than ever, parents must become active participants in their children's education. And by that I don't mean simply that they must complain about the "child-care crisis." Parents must increase their own parenting skills and also pay closer attention to the surrogate care being given to their children. While I don't pretend that CLC is the only school offering quality care for young children, it does provide a uniquely effective model. I hope that by focusing on the strategies CLC has developed, parents will gain insights into ways to improve their own interactions with their children and will have a yardstick by which to measure day-care facilities they may be considering. I believe passionately that we need to develop an army of educated advocates for our children. I hope that this book will contribute in some way, however small, to that end.

The CLC strategies we will be discussing provide the framework for meeting individual children's special needs and developing their talents. They are not difficult and they can be used easily by parents and teachers. Most importantly, they provide practical ways to preserve a child's natural self-esteem and they teach parents and teachers how to respond to children so that they as adults do not damage this fragile, innate, risk-taking link to learning.

In the following chapters we will see how these strategies evolved and how they operate during a typical school day at CLC. Then we will examine each strategy individually. But first, a few basics.

2

A Few Basics

I had no idea when I began the Early Learning Center how truly wonderful children are. They are so clear, so inventive, so free, and so worthy of our trust. After twenty years I was still thrilled every morning when I saw the first car rounding the bend carrying its precious cargo to the school. Their eyes shone with anticipation and sparkled with the joy of discovery as they spilled into the school. Watching them, I felt a surge of energy and excitement. I couldn't wait to see what they were going to learn and what they were going to teach me each day.

That attitude of expectancy was (and still is) shared by

all the adults at CLC. We never saw ourselves as instructors, caretakers, or even worse, policemen, but as helpers and fellow learners. We wanted to say to each student, "Child, you have a lot inside you and we want to help you focus that in a way that makes sense and that will help make the world make sense for you."

The key that enabled us to unlock this hidden potential in each child is respect. It's a simple principle grounded in an ancient truth, "treat others as you would like to be treated." But treating children with this kind of respect is not an automatic response. Too often we practice the inverse of that truth, treating others as we were treated.

Fortunately, most of us were treated by the adults in our lives as human beings. We were taken seriously, responded to, dealt with in a reasonable manner. That's the natural way for people to be with other people, whether they're parents with children, or friends with friends.

But I think we all remember times when the response we got seemed hurtful or curt or without understanding. We retain images from our childhood of moments when we were not being heard, received, welcomed, or approved of, when it seemed we were being treated as an object, a target for emotions which belonged to other relationships. You may remember having been treated or talked to as if you were not a whole person—as if you were a doll or a pet, someone who couldn't be allowed to make decisions and whose ideas and feelings were dismissed as "childish" and therefore, by definition, unworthy of serious consideration.

We responded strongly to those situations. When a parent criticized us for making a mistake, we didn't feel quite so confident about risking something new again. When a teacher embarrassed us in front of the class, we lost interest in what she was teaching. We reacted strongly to adult disapproval because we took adults seriously. Children do the same with us today. The least we can do is reciprocate.

I have warmer memories of childhood, too, of course. I remember my father's wonderfully kind attention and how he and I used to sing together—as literal an expression of harmony between two persons as I can think of. It's no wonder that I've often sung in a church choir, or that I pop the cassette of Mozart's "Requiem" into the car stereo when I'm on a long drive. You see, I have those moments of song within me. I think that singing was natural for my father and I'm grateful for having been a part of it. But maybe the most important thing about it was that through the singing he accepted me as a person who could share fully in something he liked to do.

Psychologist Harry Stack Sullivan, one of the great figures in American psychology, said that the kind of person you are depends a lot on the balance of approval and disapproval you lived with as a child. Children try to do what's expected of them, and when they're approved of it means they're succeeding in being part of the world of adults. Success of that kind is tremendously important. But sometimes, doing what's expected of you is very hard. Let me tell about one of the children at the school, whom I'll call Jackie.

It is Jackie's first day at school. She's a pretty, bright child just past two, coming into the school her brother attended a few years ago. Her parents want her to be in the school and she wants to do what's expected of her. But it's the first day in a brand-new situation, really her first adventure away from home and mother, on her own. It's all a little overwhelming. I hear her moaning—not quite crying—"My mommy, my mommy" over and over again. What shall I do?

One response would be to gather her up and cuddle and rock her, telling her that it's really all right. I've had teachers in the school who would do just that. Another would be to tell her firmly to "stop crying and go play" with some of the other children, and fortunately, I've not had teachers who would respond that way, for it's tantamount to saying her feelings aren't legitimate. A third response would be to ignore her behavior and pretend that everything's fine, which I think she would interpret as ignoring her. I mention these ways of responding because I think you're familiar with all of them—familiar because they are *familial* responses, part of family life. I responded in another way.

I went to Jackie and sat beside her on our carpeted floor and put one arm loosely around her, just so she'd know I was there. Other children came by and I talked briefly with them, but I kept that arm around Jackie. I said to her, "You wish your mommy were here?" She cried a little more, then quieted down a bit. I reached behind me for one of the Montessori letters which are so basic in the school—letters six inches high, cut out of felt, and glued to smooth, white plastic tablets. Then I guided Jackie's finger to trace the felt letter, as the simplest introduction to what school is about—to take her for a moment out of the inner world of Mommy into the outer world of ELC. We started to build a bridge. Our business, as teachers and parents, has so much to do with building bridges from one moment of experience to others, from fragmentary concepts to whole structures of thought, from the here and now of home and school to the wide world of time and space.

I was watching this incident on videotape later with a friend. The friend said, "How unhappy that child seems. Have you been able to do anything about it?" I thought of Jackie as she'd been from the second or third day of school—joyful, busy, discovering things, running in eagerly in the morning with hardly a nod to the greeter, hardly a backward glance to her mother. *How important is context*, I thought—the whole picture, not just the isolated moment. How important for that whole may be that moment. I do not wish to say that what I did is the right or the prescribed thing to do when a child cries for its mother. I do say that one must respond as one human being to another, that Jackie, or anyone else, is trying at any moment to do the best she or he can at that moment, in that situation, and that *this* is something to respect.

Respecting the Child As an Individual

A word about the first response I mentioned—the cuddling and rocking. It is a decent and human response, but I don't think it makes for what I call a "growing moment." It's a response which may insulate the child from the world rather than helping her accept the reality of her feelings and of the world in which they are occurring. The triple elements of comfort, acceptance, and action, which I tried to include in my response, seem to have been present at important moments in my own childhood.

Taking children seriously, respecting them as individuals, then, is the most important basic of building self-esteem in our children. The second is recognizing that behavior is a whole in which feelings and actions, inseparable from each other, are also inseparable from our individual histories and the culture we share. People make a lot of errors and suffer a lot of unnecessary guilt because they don't recognize that. We tend to take behavior as something isolated, or tied to immediate circumstances.

Some years ago Julie came to school one day and within half an hour she was getting the worst of it in a hair-pulling brawl with Liz. One of the staff separated them and gave Liz the standard fifteen-second lecture. "I can't let you do that; children aren't for hitting. Let me help you find some work."

At the staff meeting, the staff talked about Liz, wondering what we could do to help her better understand how to solve interpersonal problems, and what had been going on in the school that brought about this fight. I talked about Julie, not Liz, about her great skill at manipulating other children.

"She set it up for Liz to hit her," I said. "She was acting out a situation at home. Her older sister does just the same thing to her that she was doing to Liz. Julie and her parents are the ones to work with."

Ron intervened the next time Julie went on a rampage. He pointed out to her how she'd managed to get another child—this time it was Suzy—to shove her so she could shove back. He suggested that this was behavior which disturbed him and others, and which he could not allow. Importantly, he told her that he felt she was angry and that it was all right to be angry. He said he hoped she would think of why she was angry and with whom she was angry. He also told her he liked her spunkiness and appreciated her work in the school and that there was work to do with him now.

Of course, that won't solve the problem. Her history is one involving a lot of envy, rivalry, and imitation of her older sister and a good deal of jealousy toward her younger brother. Traditionally the "sandwich" child has this kind of problem, the need to act out both aggression and guilt. A culture in which lines of authority and responsibility are unclear adds to the problem. All of this generates feelings of frustration, ambivalence, anger, and depression. So Julie's reactions aren't just isolated fragments of difficult behavior. They belie feelings, a history, membership in a culture.

You know better than anyone else the history of your children and the culture of which they are a part and the feelings they exhibit day by day. Or do you? Sometimes the things we're closest to are the things it's hardest for us to recognize. Because we're within them; we're part of them. Our children, you know, are very much like us. You may object and say, no, they are exactly the opposite. That may be true regarding surface attitudes and actions, but every coin has two sides and the fact that one is up doesn't erase the existence of the other nor alter the fact that they are obverse sides of the same coin. As the cultural anthropologist Jules Henry points out, that coin is the legal tender within a particular and unique family—whichever side is showing.

This points out the difficulty in responding as "just one human being to another." Human beings—be they parents, children or teachers—are infinitely varied. Variety is the spice of life and the glory of God, but it makes nonsense out of universal rules and dictates that much of education and a lot of being a parent will always be more art than science. Art deals with the unique, with the perfect pattern that fits just one set of circumstances—with actions, and feelings inseparable from each other and from a personal history and culture. Your particular family and how you bring your children up is as special, different, and precious a thing as a Beethoven quartet, or ought to be. And yet, as poets and philosophers have told us over the centuries, we need principles and predictabilities. That's why I can make lists of basic principles to improve early-childhood education, prefacing them with the warning that everyone is different, but believing something much harder: that in some very subtle and enormously important ways, everyone is alike.

One of the fundamental ways in which we are most alike is in our need for recognition and appreciation. At CLC, one staff person is assigned every morning to greet each child and let him or her know how much he or she is valued and welcomed. Because everything about the school is so supportive, people often asked when I was there, "Can't you take it for granted that the children feel welcome?"

My answer was yes and no. I think you must never take people's feelings for granted. We know this to be true in adult situations—isn't it one of the most frequent complaints about marriages, that spouses take each other too much for granted? Children are less verbal in telling us about this, or perhaps they haven't learned the appropriate words yet, but they feel it too. Thus, another basic is: *express your positive feelings about your children openly and often*. At CLC we learned to make our support and welcome clear and explicit. As parents, we need to do the same thing.

As I see it, the aim of all education, whether at home or at school, is to create a kind of situation in which both children and parents can be themselves, at their best. We talk about this in terms of "quiet confidence," which means that a child is secure enough, sure enough about the place and the people to work as a researcher in the various learning activities that make up our program. We certainly didn't succeed 100 percent in helping children feel this security—some of our children's home situations accompanied them into the school and may have become the determining element in some of their activities, which were neither quiet nor, as we saw them, marked by much confidence. I don't want to suggest that letting children know they're important, supported, cared about, and loved is the complete answer to children's early needs. But we live in a culture in which it seems easier to say no than yes, in which many of us are harried enough by our work, and anxious enough about our lives in general, that we forget to say and act out the positive feelings we have toward our children.

Three Pluses —and a Wish

A dozen or more years ago I was introduced to a theory about human behavior called Synectics. I learned from it that our feedback to children, and to each other as teachers, is most successful when it includes what we like about someone's behavior as well as what we'd like to see changed or stopped. Our shorthand for this became "three pluses and a wish." But it doesn't really matter what we call it. What matters is that we are always on the lookout for the positive things about children—their venturing, their persistence, their imagination, how they share their interests with other children, how much they learn on their own.

These positive things provide a context for what we believe might be or even must be changed. I mentioned Jackie before, a two-year-old new to the school, who spent some of her first morning moaning for her mommy and then turned into one of our happiest, busiest children. Several weeks after that incident, I found a moment with her and said something like this—"Jackie, I like the way you just built the pink tower. You saw that the smaller pieces go on top of the larger pieces. You had each piece right in the center of the piece below it. I do wish that you'd put the pieces away now that you're through working with them, so that other children can find and use them."

When I tell about an incident like that, someone is sure to ask me why I didn't just tell Jackie to put the things away—politely, pleasantly, but firmly. But that would make it appear that the function of the teacher is to demand and disapprove; and it would imply, too, that the most appropriate place for learning materials is on the shelf, rather than on the floor or the table being used. (Parenthetically, I wonder how many parents you know have a similar attitude about toys, or at least, who communicate that attitude whether they truly feel it or not.) My positive statements told Jackie how much I really did appreciate her love for active learning, and it was in that context—very genuinely as part of that appreciation— that I hoped she would learn to put things back where they lived, where the other children had come to expect them to be.

This example illustrates another basic: *even when we*

correct children, we must do so in a way that builds their self-esteem, not belittles it. This is one of the ways we show support for children, and at the same time play an essentially adult role. As adults we have the responsibility of helping children modify their thinking and behaving, of helping them explore possibilities and accept the fact that other persons have different ideas and values, and that that doesn't necessarily make anyone right or wrong, good or bad. Whether it's at home or at school, the adults who are close to children have both to be supportive and to help with growth and development, recognizing that the two are not separate from, and certainly not antagonistic to, each other.

I think that both as parents and teachers we too often see ourselves as value givers in fundamentally negative terms. There are abundant reasons for that deep in our Judeo-Christian tradition. Goodness, particularly the supreme goodness, is ineffable, to be known by inspiration or revelation; but it is not something we can objectively describe. The basic directives which underlie that tradition are sometimes referred to as the "thou shalt nots." And our linguistic philosophy, developed over the centuries, tells us that we venture into a wilderness when we try to say what that is, but are on stable ground when we define something in terms of what it is not. Add to that a quality which may be related to our own freebooting economic and social history, made alive for me recently when a captain of industry said, "Every American has the God-given right to say no."

We do say a lot of no's. Even if we don't use that monosyllable, we say no in our attitudes, our comments, our gestures. When a mother in the supermarket grabs her child by the back of his shirt collar and jerks him away from the comic books, she says no far more loudly than she could shout it. But beyond this basic negative—one of the first "words" a child learns—are the many subtle

A Few Basics

negations of the child's worth. All of these negations, whether spoken or unspoken, are intended, I'm sure, to spur Jimmy or Judy or Jane on to goodness. But they all carry a message of irritation, frustration, impatience, disapproval, and rejection. Just listen! I do.

Many times I've heard a mother yelling at her child through the open car door as the kid rushed—it seemed— to the haven of the Children's Learning Center. "Say good morning," she screeched. Later, in a parent conference, she told me, "I do so wish Mary Lou would learn some of the common courtesies."

I tried to explain to her that one doesn't teach courtesy by yelling angrily at children—or even telling them sweetly to say thank you. One doesn't help them build that sense of worth out of which they, as worthy individuals, can relate beautifully to other individuals, by treating them as if they were unworthy.

Another parent greeted his son Jules with, "So, did you go on crying all morning?" The father hoped (he would tell me if I asked him) that Jules would be brave enough and strong enough and resilient enough—and on and on—not to be a crybaby, because crybabies have a hard time in this world. What came out to Jules was that he made his father ashamed of him, that the things that really bothered him weren't important, and that tears were definitely not okay.

If the balance between approval and disapproval shapes personality, I think we're way overbalanced on the disapproval end of things. It takes a long time—maybe more time than there is—for a child to overcome the sense of having been told, in one way or another, day after day, what he interprets as "you're no good."

We have a lot to do with the kind of living from which, and through and in which, our children learn life. And we have to understand that learning and living are inextricably intertwined. A quote from *The Inner Game of*

Skiing illustrates what educators and psychologists have known for a long time. "When my son Otis is exposed to an unfamiliar skill, he will watch what is going on for a few minutes with total concentration. Wide-eyed, he simply gawks, absorbing the entire image at once, without breaking it down into its separate parts. A child doesn't segment experience. He doesn't learn linearally, he learns holistically. With a quiet and open mind, he takes in whole images, not just visual images, but 'feelages' as well. With his concentration focused, he acquires a *feel* for what he is *seeing.*"

The author goes on to say, "the quality of learning is directly proportionate to the quality of feedback a person receives from experience," and notes that the feedback depends on a kind of awareness which lies in quietness— in what, I think he would agree, we call "quiet confidence." Thus, holistic learning is important. Life is a whole, not something you can break down into parts or activities. It is all of your life that has meaning, and all of a child's life through which meaning comes to him. To quote the early progressive educators, life is learned in the living of it. What kind of living are our children learning? Is it living in which, self-worth is high, communication is direct, clear, specific and honest; rules are flexible, human, open and hopeful? I sense that is the kind of life from which Johnny bounces into school so happily, ready for whatever the day may bring, greeting me as happily as I greet him. It is clear to me that it is not everybody's life.

What if, indeed, learning comes in wholes, not in separate lessons? What if attitudes and behaviors, functioning intelligence, responsibility, social concern, and the ability—in the "generative" adult years—to live well with one's own children are learned in wholes in that basic educational institution, the home? What does that mean for us as educators, both teachers and parents?

Our children shape themselves on our behavior.

Our children want to live up to our expectations.

What kind of feedback do we have on how we behave with them and toward them, within their hearing and observation?

How much are we aware of that which we expect from them, and wish about them?

These are questions to which each of us does need answers. I cannot give them to you. But I hope that in this book we may be able to discover some of them together.

3

A Day at the Children's
Learning Center

One of the greatest educators of this century stumbled onto education as I did, quite by accident. In 1904, Maria Montessori became the first woman to graduate from the University of Rome as a doctor. Finding no physicians in Rome who wanted a woman for a partner and no hospitals that would admit her to their staffs, she finally accepted a position as a doctor in a public housing development. In 1904, there were no x-rays or computerized diagnostic equipment. Dr. Montessori's most valuable diagnostic tools were her keen powers of observation. As she moved in and out of the slums of Rome, becoming intrigued with the children who lived there, she spent many hours observing them. She studied how they interacted with each other and how they learned with almost no educational materials. Her observations eventually led her to develop her own learning materials and her own method of education. She saw her pedagogy as an offering to educators so that they could "elevate the intelligence of man."

The strategies of the Children's Learning Center are definitely rooted in Montessori's methods, although we also borrowed liberally from two other sources—the Leicestershire Schools in England and Synectics, Inc. We used materials from all three of these sources along with others that we discovered and created ourselves through the years. I can think of no better way to illustrate how we put these strategies and materials to work than by creating an imaginary day for you, pulling from memory examples involving children I have taught.

At 8:45 A.M., cars begin pulling up in the school's circular driveway. The staff member who has been designated as the "Greeter" for the day opens the car doors and welcomes the children. With a quick "'bye Mom," they zip across the driveway toward the school. As they reach the door they look into a big room with glass windows where they can see all the low shelves lined with interesting learning materials.

Each child opens the door himself and goes and finds his coat hook, which is easy to identify because it is color coded with his picture and his name written above it. He hangs his own coat up, just as you do when you go to your office in the morning. And just as most adults have a morning routine they follow, whether it is getting a cup of coffee from the cafeteria or making the rounds, greeting their co-workers, children do too. They have their own morning rituals. Some head straight for the snack bar to get a glass of natural apple juice and hang out with their friends for a few minutes; others who are not so sociable first thing in the morning get a book and climb up into the reading loft, while the most gregarious race outside to clamber on the real lobster boat anchored in our backyard.

By 9:30 A.M., everyone has arrived and the school day has officially begun. But, unlike regular schools, there are no bells, no periods, no teachers issuing instructions. The children move freely around choosing the materials and activities that interest them. The atmosphere sparkles with the excitement of a Christmas morning, for a variety of beautiful, intriguing, toy-like objects await them, and the children go to them eagerly. Several youngsters are chattering around a hill of blocks that they have begun to assemble into some kind of structure. Four-year-old Joey sprawls on his tummy, already deep in concentration as he matches wooden cylinders to holes in long, wooden blocks. Brad and Matthew, who are fast becoming friends, are fitting together large plastic pieces that will form a puppet stage. Two-year-old Sharon is industriously washing down a table. All of the children have become involved on their own. The teachers sit on the floor, at eye level with the children, always available to help, to introduce new materials, often suggesting an activity or a lesson, but never insisting, allowing each child to concentrate on the work he has chosen.

We always referred to the children's activities as work, not play, because each is a learning experience and, however enjoyable, constitutes work to the children. Noted child psychologist Bruno Bettelheim confirmed this in an article in the *Atlantic Monthly*. Contrary to what adults often assume, Bettelheim observed that a child does not play spontaneously only to while away the time. Play is the child's most useful tool for preparing himself for the future and its tasks. It teaches the child, without his being aware of it, the habits most needed for intellectual

Children are "invited" to learn by this space.

growth, such as stick-to-itiveness, which is so important in all learning.*

Bettelheim concluded that if perseverance does not become a habit through what is enjoyable, it is not likely to become one through an endeavor like schoolwork. Calling our children's activities work is one more way we show our respect for them.

The overall environment of the CLC represents one of the most basic principles of Montessori, freedom— freedom to learn. Children are inquisitive, fascinated with the world, eager to try things out. Given freedom, they learn a great deal on their own and with each other's help, and perhaps learn it better. Each child does what he is ready to do, at his own pace, in his own way, which goes a long way toward making learning meaningful and

* *Atlantic Monthly,* March 1987, pp. 35–46.

effective. I have observed that the more adults stand over children, directing them, quizzing them, judging them or scolding them, the less children will learn through their own curiosity or need. What they learn in those circumstances—and this is much, I'm afraid, of the learning which goes on in the schools I described in chapter 1—is how to deal with demanding and punitive adults. Children at CLC are never pressured to perform, or peppered with questions. We adopted the motto, "teach, don't test," as one of our basic communication strategies.

Just as children are free to move around within the classroom, so they may also go outside whenever they choose. Visitors are often amazed by this practice. "If I let my class go out whenever they wanted to, they'd be out playing all the time!" a visiting teacher said, her tone of voice implying as much criticism as her statement. There's an assumption in her statement, which is very common, that children only learn in structured academic environments and only when they are forced to.

My assumption is that children are desperate to learn and will learn almost anyplace where we give them the opportunity. CLC considers the outdoors to be a part of the school, not an escape from it. Everywhere on the grounds wonderful science lessons are waiting to be discovered. There are funny-looking bugs to examine, trees with different texture barks to feel and compare, leaves of all shapes and colors to match and a rich variety of sights, sounds, and smells to identify and enjoy. The children also learn important lessons in interaction with the varied ages and backgrounds of the children as they play outdoors.

Occasionally a youngster will spend what seems like an inordinate amount of time outside, but when that happens there is usually a reason. I am reminded of an experiment done with babies in an orphanage several years ago. The babies were offered a variety of foods and were allowed to choose what they wanted and how much they wanted to eat. The researchers discovered that while the babies might occasionally binge on a particular food, over the course of a month they ate a perfectly balanced diet. I think that is what educators and parents need to remember when they become concerned that a child seems to be focusing on one activity too much. We need to take a longer view of a child's activities than just this day, this week, or even this month.

I firmly believe that giving children this kind of freedom pays off. Visitors were always saying they'd never seen such peaceful, relaxed children. Furthermore, most of the school's students achieve beyond their grade levels, so unrestricted outdoor time obviously did not hinder their academic progress.

Another aspect of this freedom to move in or out that often concerns observers, is that the CLC staff does not insist on having a teacher outside monitoring the children at all times. The building has huge windows that extend all the way to the floor, so it is easy for us to keep an eye on the children. We discovered that when we trusted children to take care of themselves they responded by behaving responsibly. Watch any schoolyard and you will see that children take bigger risks and fight with each other more if a teacher is watching. They know that she is there to stop them. It seems that they take fewer risks when they know they are on their own.

"But what if a child runs out without his coat?" some observers worry. That does happen. But usually, the child discovers for himself how uncomfortable the chilly air can be (the best kind of learning!) and he comes right back in—either to stay or to get his coat. However, staff members are alert to the possibility of a child's being so intent on his activity that he will not notice the cold. Then they remind him to put on his coat.

I often feel we are too concerned about how well a child is bundled up. Sensory experience from the earliest

Learning happens inside and outside.

months of a child's life stimulates his mental development. Yet what do we do to a baby who needs to see and
hear and feel? We zip him into a snowsuit so bulky that he
can hardly move. We cover his head with a cap and add a
visor so as to protect his eyes from the sun. Then we put
him into a baby carriage and pull down the hood to block
the sunlight. Finally, we hang a little plastic bauble in
front of the baby's face so he will have something to look
at while he is outside. And then we wonder why our children are so restricted in their thinking.

There are many other ways that we baby our children
unnecessarily. Yet certain habits, especially in school,
have become so ingrained that we don't even question
them. One is the custom of having a supervised snack
time each morning. That's simply one more way in which
we deny children respect as individuals. When there is
only one time allowed for snacking, everyone has to be
hungry or thirsty at the same time.

Think what it means to us adults to be able to eat or
drink something almost whenever we choose. We don't
have to wait until everyone else in our office wants a cup
of coffee before we can get one. If a child is thirsty, why
should he have to wait to get a cup of apple juice? At the
Children's Learning Center, juice and crackers are available all morning, so the children may help themselves at
any time. The system works beautifully. The children feel
in charge of their own needs, and they don't abuse the
privilege. If there is an occasional spill, the child gets
a little bucket and sponge nearby and cleans it up.
At home, Mom or Dad can set aside a low table in the
kitchen for a child, and place on it a little basket of fruit
or crackers in an easy-to-open container. A tiny pail of
water with a sponge in it can be placed under the sink
every morning and the little one can be given the responsibility of cleaning up his own accidents. You will find
him doing it willingly.

As important as it is for our children to be able to move about freely, to eat when they want and to choose their own activities, there is one other freedom which is equally important, and that is the freedom to simply do nothing. Children don't have to be busy every minute. In fact, it's even okay for a child to be bored from time to time.

Occasionally a visitor to the school would come up to me and say, "Well, Mrs. Skutch," (which let me know right away that they were unhappy, since everyone called me Margaret) "I saw that child just doing nothing for ten minutes and no teacher went over to her." I'd just smile and say, "Yes, isn't it wonderful?" By and large, children aren't allowed much time to watch and think in our culture. They have to look busy. But a lot of creativity happens out of rumination. The biographies of creative people are filled with stories of long hours they spent sitting by a river as teenagers, thinking their own thoughts, roaming through the woods with their faithful dog, or in quiet prayer. What child has time to do this today? We rush our children from one activity to another, from scout meetings to Little League to music lessons, leaving them little time to simply be themselves. In fact, as Bettelheim notes, they are continually distracted from the task of self-discovery, forced to develop their talents and personalities as those who are in charge of the various activities think best. At CLC we never wanted to deprive children of the leisure time needed to develop a rich inner life.

Structure Is in the Teacher's Mind

Of course, that doesn't mean that teachers don't observe and interact with the children. They do, constantly. They show a genuine interest in them as individuals, offering help and gently guiding them to activities appropriate to their needs and level of development. Furthermore, they see that each child receives at least one individual, in-depth lesson each day. Much planning goes into what the teachers do; while, to the child, the atmosphere feels free and unstructured, there is a great deal of structuring from each teacher's point of view. Still, some of the best learning comes in unplanned, unexpected ways, as I discovered one morning.

On this particular day I decided that I was not in the mood to teach. I wanted very much to do some drawing. I saw the attribute blocks (a set of plastic blocks varying in shape, size, color, and thickness) and put them together in a design on the floor. I then began to transfer the outline of the shapes to a piece of paper. Kendall, age six, had joined me as I began tracing and by the time I was adding color four other children were seated around me. The children were looking at my picture and telling each other what images it made them think of. After each child told what they thought mine looked like, they asked if they could join. I told them that they were all welcome and only needed to find a pencil and paper. The discussion that ensued from the images of my picture included the scientific explanation of an echo, and the myths about Echo and Mercury. I acted out the myth about Echo in which I made sure to get the last word after each of the children had spoken. Finally, one child yelled that he had gotten the picture and would I please stop. The "lesson" ended with all of us laughing at what a silly echo I was.

My initial interest in my drawing, in the shapes and colors I was using, apparently attracted the interest of some children. I was intrigued at their images which were sparked by my picture, "a dog from the land of triangles," "a fish," "a city of buildings"—and I was delighted that they were willing to share these images.

During that "lesson" the children learned about shapes, color, Greek myths, and a little bit about how sound behaves. What I feel is even more important is what those children learned about me. They learned I am a person who enjoys drawing and colors. They learned that they

51

The author with a child. Two-year-olds *can* read.

may see one thing in a drawing and I may see another, and that that's okay. They also learned that I could be silly in a dramatization and that I derived pleasure out of their interest and excitement. Another important lesson they learned is that if I can be silly so can they. If I am willing to share my images with them, it's okay for them to share with others. I believe that what happened in that session between the children and me is what George Dennison, author of *The Lives of Children,* calls the reality of encounter. Dennison maintains that:

> There is no such thing as learning except (as Dewey tells us) in the continuum of experience. But this

52

continuum cannot survive in the classroom unless there is reality of encounter between adults and the children. The teachers must be themselves and not play roles. They must teach the children and not teach "subjects."

That's the goal of all our interactions with children at CLC, whether they are impromptu sessions like my art experiment, or the daily in-depth lessons.

The Prepared Environment

Another goal is to provide what Montessori called "the prepared environment." In planning and furnishing the Children's Learning Center we tried to create a space that would respond to the child's needs for freedom of movement, comfort, and security while displaying beautiful, interesting materials in ways that would call out to them to come and learn. The learning materials that Montessori created are the most essential part of this environment. Designed in a preplastic era, they are mostly made of wood which is finely sanded, dove-tailed and either varnished or painted. Children are so used to lightweight plastic that they are intrigued by the feel and weight of the wooden objects. They rarely throw the pieces around or show disrespect for them the way they do their toys. They seem to understand that they are tools for learning, and treat them as we do, like precious jewels. One young boy went home after his first day at the school and told his mother proudly, "there aren't any toys there!"

The Montessori tools are precisely designed to help a child visualize a specific concept. And logically, each learning material extends a child's experience, building progressively from one level of conceptualization to another.

You can see how this works by watching Brock as he experiments with the wooden cylinder blocks. This activity is new to him, yet because the set includes only wooden blocks with holes of various diameters and wooden cylinders similar in size to the holes, it is natural for him to insert the cylinders in the holes. By matching the cylinders to the holes, he finds there is a place for every cylinder. He feels satisfaction in successfully putting each cylinder into the proper hole and he gains confidence because he has been able to fit the pieces together without help from a teacher. He will have the self-assurance to risk trying an activity on his own again.

Across the room, Suzanne is experimenting with another set of Montessori materials—sound cylinders. She picks up one red-topped wooden cylinder, holds it to her ear and shakes it, listening carefully. She puts it down, picks up a similar looking black-topped cylinder and shakes it, hoping it will match the sound of the first cylinder. Suzanne is learning to use the scientific approach, working like a researcher looking for the answer to a puzzling problem.

The cylinder blocks and sound cylinder blocks teach children an important concept—matching. Learning comes from building on whatever is already known. In order to make sense of new information, the child must search his mind for corresponding information that is already understood. By matching pieces in a set, he is training his brain to think this way.

Another valuable concept taught by the Montessori materials is grading. Bobby is learning grading as he works with the brown rectangular prisms called the "broad stairs." Spreading the ten prisms around him on the floor, he starts with the widest prism and adds progressively narrower ones to create a staircase. He is learning the concept of wide to narrow. After successfully putting four prisms in place, he realizes that each of the prisms becomes narrower by the same amount of difference. He looks for a fifth block that will be smaller by the

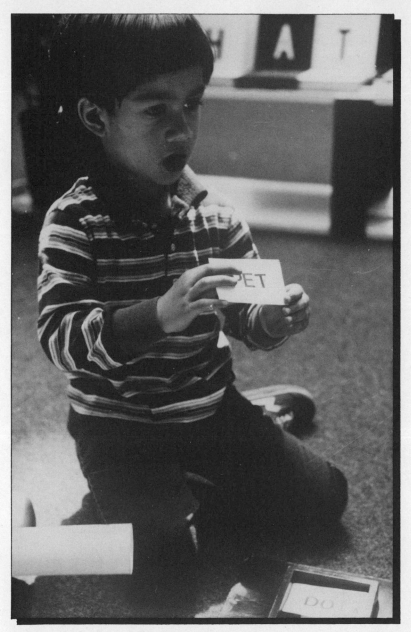

Children teach one another.

same amount. Other materials teach the gradations of thick to thin, or large to small, or heavy to light and a full range of colors.

In another corner, Greg and Nancy are tasting something from separate containers. They are discovering an interesting variation on the grading exercise, as they dip plain boiled pasta into a variety of condiments ranging from tart mustard, to tangy ketchup, to sweet honey. There are also containers that have spices, or other pungent substances to be categorized according to smell.

The sense of touch gets attention too, as you can see by the pieces of sandpaper with varying degrees of roughness on a table nearby. There are soundmakers too: bells, whistles, and xylophones that make the children aware of pitch, color, and tone. Cymbals, blocks, and drums invite experimentation with rhythm and volume.

You may suspect that there is more than matching or grading going on with all these activities. The children are also developing their five senses. Montessori believed that such stimulation awakens all areas of the brain. She saw learning and memory as multifaceted, with various perceptions reinforcing others. Have you ever noticed that a certain smell suddenly encountered can take you immediately back to a childhood experience, calling to memory all of the accompanying sights and sounds of that experience? We found the sense of touch worked as a wonderful reinforcement when our children were learning the alphabet. We had them trace with their fingers large textured letters glued on colored Plexiglass, while at the same time we said to them, "this is 'buh,'" (being careful to keep the consonant sounds in our mouths, not using our vocal chords except with vowels). Thus they were getting a multisensory impact, seeing the letter, feeling it, and hearing us say it at the same time.

One of Montessori's most innovative ideas was the development of "practical life activities." She observed that children between the ages of two and three have a great interest in order and cleanliness. They enjoy activities that require following a series of sequential steps, and they receive tremendous satisfaction in accomplishing practical, "real-world" tasks. Thus, on any morning, you can find several children intently working in our practical-life area. Today, Katie is offering several other children the carrot she has carefully sliced and arranged on a plate. John, proud of his shiny brown shoes, is neatly putting the polish away. (We use polish in a neutral color. Now, almost all of the children wear sneakers, so we keep an extra leather shoe around just so they can learn how to polish their shoes.) Susan is setting the table. Children will often spend hours repeating one of these simple tasks. They are not working to please a teacher or even to clean the shoes, but they are totally absorbed in the process. Developing these practical skills gives them a tremendous sense of security and self-confidence.

Despite the importance of Montessori methods and materials at the school, it was only in the beginning that we called it a Montessori school. That name no longer fits, since we incorporated many additional methods and materials.

The Leicestershire Schools

In the late sixties, I learned about an educational movement that grew out of the schools in Leicestershire, England. The Plowdon Report had aroused the interest and excitement of American educators by its description of the innovative educational methods being developed by these schools. In the Leicestershire schools the children were given the same kind of liberty with limits that Montessori advocates. They were not seated in rows, "pinned like butterflies to their desks." They were free to move around, and learning was individualized. They were not directed in every movement, but were free to study those things that interested them. The reports said that the children in these schools performed better on standardized tests and had more academic success than children in traditional schools.

In 1968 I received a grant to visit the Leicestershire schools to see firsthand the exciting things they were doing; and later, some of those educators came to ELC. I found that, indeed, the schools in Leicestershire County did provide a very intense and high-quality form of teaching and, like Montessori, gave children lots of high-quality didactic materials from which to learn.

One of the things I appreciated most about the Leicestershire schools was the quality of their staff interaction. Each school principal was autonomous; no central committee dictated curriculum to him. He had a much more interesting and dynamic job than most school principals in the United States seem to have, and he took a great deal of personal responsibility for the quality of learning in his school.

The teachers also had a wonderful camaraderie that I have seldom experienced in this country. The talk in the teacher's room always reflected their deep care and concern for the children. The teachers, especially in the elementary school, emphasized the pluses of their students and avoided the kind of negative "flagging" that seems to occur so often in American schools, where a child gets labeled a troublemaker or a poor learner in the first grade and carries that negative label throughout his school career. The quality of these staff meetings inspired me to enhance our own staff sessions and to expand our coaching strategies.

I was also impressed with the quality of the learning materials that the Leicestershire schools developed. I brought back quantities of brightly colored, durable plastic materials that helped children learn logical, linguistic, and mathematical concepts. The wooden Dienes blocks, which are very similar to Montessori's golden beads, are a good example. They can be used in a number of teaching games to help children learn to count, add, subtract, multiply, and divide. I loved the balance beam with weights hung on either side of the fulcrum. It enables children to learn addition in a very graphic way. For example, a weight hung under the numeral two and another under four on one side will balance with a weight hung under the numeral six. With the help of these materials, we frequently see four- and five-year-olds doing math on a second- or third-grade level. These two materials can also be used with students up through the fourth or fifth grade.

Some of our best problem-solving materials came from the Far West Laboratories for Educational Research and Development in San Francisco, and were developed by Dr. Glenn Nimnicht and the staff there. He worked closely with me at ELC, consulting on the Follow Through Program for Head Start. With these materials, the child must use logic to predict the unknown.

For example, with pattern cards, the child watches a long card with symbols in a particular pattern being pulled from a box. As the symbols come into view, he is asked by the teacher to predict the next symbol, based on the pattern so far. When the child becomes comfortable with one matrix pattern, the teacher can set up a different one in a tic-tac-toe design, or the teacher can ask the child to create his own pattern. This activity is a favorite one with both children and parents. After watching me demonstrate a matrix lesson, one father protested, "I just went to Harvard and spent $2,000 for four days to learn that and you're teaching it to my three-year-old!" I often got teased that I was teaching children to take college entrance exams when they were two. I'm glad if our students did do well on standardized exams; however, the important issue was not teaching them to take tests, but teaching them to think through problems.

TAKING CHILDREN SERIOUSLY

Parents may be interested to know that while learning materials like these are mainly promoted for schools, they can also be ordered for a child's use at home. At the end of this book, in an appendix, I am including names and addresses of companies that make the materials I have described, so that catalogues may be ordered. Some of the simpler materials you can also make yourself. For example, to make a matrix card, buy a large piece of posterboard and draw nine blocks on it. Then cut sponges into one-inch squares, using three colored sponges. In the first vertical column, put one, two, three orange sponge pieces. In the second column, put one, two, three blue pieces; and in the third, put one, two, three red pieces.

I don't like games that emphasize memorization. That's why, to me, the matrix is such an exciting learning tool. It helps children learn to think and predict. I don't want children to memorize. I want them to see that nothing is too hard to be unlocked by thinking and problem solving. I want them to realize that if they look hard enough, the data is all there.

One of the most recent additions to CLC has been an Apple computer. The Logo program is especially good because of the open-ended opportunities it offers the child to be creative and solve problems. Even the two-year-olds can operate the computer, which is so popular that it is always in use. Recently, the school has added several new computer programs, including IBM's "Writing to Read."

At 11:30, Bach's violin concerto goes on the stereo. The children know that is the signal to begin cleaning up their work area and putting materials away. The mornings go by so quickly it is always surprising when the music begins. It can't be time to go yet! When cleanup is finished, everyone gathers for a few minutes of dance or exercise. After a full morning of concentration, they all enjoy this chance to be silly and to release tension. Today Brian, the Head Teacher, leads a spirited game of Follow the Leader.

60

A Day at the Children's Learning Center

Computers are so popular, they are always in use. CLC Director Maureen Murphy watches a young learner solve a problem.

If the weather is nice the staff might take a big parachute and enjoy dancing in it as they run through the meadow behind the school.

After exercise time, the children get ready to go home, and wait in our sunken "Forum" area for their rides to arrive. The Head Teacher tells a story, creates an impromptu puppet show with two socks, or leads a sing-along. By 12 P.M. the children are all gone, but echos of their laughter linger and the room still seems charged with their energy.

For the staff, the day does not end when the children leave. They will spend the next three hours analyzing their

61

work. With the help of the Video, and Pad-and-Pencil Coaches, they will review the things that they did well and look for ways to do them even better tomorrow. Afterward, they will record the work that they did with each student today, and make detailed plans for the next day.

At 4 P.M., after making one last check of the classroom to see that everything is ready for tomorrow, the day will be officially over. But the staff's love for children and the excitement about the ways they are helping them learn, do not end when they turn off the light and lock the door. Many nights, when I was director of the school, we sat around the big table in my country kitchen for hours after dinner sharing stimulating ideas about the wonder of working with children or discussing new methods of education with some of the educational experts who had visited the school. Although the setting has changed, the staff still regularly gets together for those dinner/discussion meetings. For most of the staff, then and now, working at the Learning Center was, and is, not a job, but a passion.

I hope you have been able to catch some of that passion in this rather broad description of the way the school works. In the next five chapters I will discuss the specific learning strategies that made working with the children so delightful for us—and for them!

Part II

FIVE LEARNING
STRATEGIES

4

Communication:
Pragmatics of Respect

The truth is that parents and teachers don't give enough thought about how they speak to children, what they say to them, and what kind of environment they create for them. And if they do think about it, they don't think of the message that the child receives. That's why communication strategy is so important. Simply, this theory allows you to put your respect for children into action. But, there is absolutely nothing simple about it!

You can show children the respect they so rightly deserve in every response you make to them. But you have to learn how. It requires rethinking your way of communicating with children as well as the environment you create for them. It isn't easy. But the payoff is enormous.

In its simplest expression, respect can be communicated in two ways: through the spoken word and through physical mannerisms. Opportunities exist at every turn to bolster children's fragile, developing self-images. As adults, we have the chance to give children what few of us were given when we were young: a healthy sense of self-worth. This may be the most important, and certainly, the most lasting gift that we can give them.

Power Wording

The spoken language is the best tool parents have to build their child's self-esteem and the most effective way for teachers to offer feedback to children. But feedback is more than just offering a positive response. The very wording of the feedback itself makes a difference in how a child perceives himself or herself. In its simplest form, language is only the sum of its smallest unit of meaning: words. And choosing the right words is all important.

Too often we speak carelessly, without thinking, using empty words or phrases. "Jimmy, you look nice this morning" we say to our young son as he comes down the stairs. There's nothing wrong with that kind of statement. We make similar ones to adults all the time. But there's nothing particularly right about it either.

Effective communication should build children's self-confidence in three ways: *by giving them credit for what they know; by expressing respect for their ability to choose; and by giving specific information about what you like or don't like about their behavior.* A better way to compliment Jimmy might be to say, "You chose a warm sweater. What good thinking on a cold day." Or you can credit Sally for combing her long hair by herself by saying, "I like the way you combed your hair to make it shine." Children, credited for their choice, are elevated in their own sight beyond belief. The message they receive is "I respect your ability to choose." The enhancement of their self-image is based on truth—not hype.

Crediting children for what they know, instead of rushing in to correct what they don't, is critical to maintaining their fragile self-esteem. If they call a horse a cat don't immediately say, "No, that's a horse." Instead try, "Johnny, you're really thinking. That animal has four legs like the cat, its ears are shaped like a cat, it's sort of the color of Mrs. Johnson's cat, and, by the way, it's a horse." In high school we learned about phyla of animals; Johnny wasn't so far wrong! He took a risk in his thinking and said, "that's a cat." He made an approximation. God gave children that ability to approximate, to take risks, to dare, but frequently we squelch that risk-taking quality through our insensitivity. So often in classrooms children will give an answer that's close, but because it's not the answer that's in the teacher's mind, it's wrong. Faced with public rejection of their idea, children shut down, and they stop making those approximate, risk-taking guesses. So, by the time they're thirty they have to go to Harvard Business School to take a course teaching them how to risk.

Because adults and eventually children become so reality-based in the precision of their thinking, they limit themselves in their potential learning. If, when faced with a problem, one censors ideas or images as being silly or far-fetched, they are eliminating a whole world of solutions. Dr. Edwin Land, whose daughter's plea was "I wish I didn't have to wait to see the photographs I take," is an excellent example of the use of imaging/wishing. It resulted in the development of the Polaroid camera and film.

In a vein similar to imaging, educator-psychologist Jean Piaget discusses the stage of intellectual development concerned with the creating of symbols. The child who looks at a potato chip and says "look, a butterfly," is retrieving his image of a butterfly. This is the beginning of abstract thinking. Piaget contends that nothing is solely copied from the external world, nor is anything completely constructed from within. He argues that the mind is best thought of not as a mechanical contrivance but rather as a creative artist. The true artist never simply copies reality nor does he merely execute some inner vision. Rather, the artist brings his experience of reality and his inner vision together by means of a creative process whose result is a product that is not reducible to its components.

Children have this "frame of reference" which they are constantly refining, expanding, and relying on for guidance. They feel the need to make pieces fit comfortably into their own puzzle, based on their prior experience with the world. If we understand this need and are not impatient with a child's leaps of logic, we can turn almost any interaction with them into an exciting opportunity for learning.

For example, Geoffrey, age six, had questioned me as to the meaning of the notation B.C. and the time that it referred to, in response to a book on dinosaurs. When I first attempted to explain it, he got stuck on the idea that zero was nothing and he could not understand how anything could be less than or go before nothing. I decided to introduce the number line to him and the idea of negative numbers. I started by explaining that although in some cases zero meant nothing or none, in other cases, it was a place holder, or a starting point. In the case of the number line it was the place that all numbers radiated from. Geoffrey stopped me and asked, "Is that the same as the way rays come out of the sun?" We talked about the sun's rays and also about how the sun is the center of our solar system. I proceeded with the lesson and used the word *negative* to refer to numbers on the left side of the number line. Geoffrey asked, "Is that like a negative from a camera?" I drew two pictures, one the negative (opposite) of the other and explained that the numbers were opposites of each other in a similar way to negatives. That image turned out to be the key which unlocked his understanding. From that one original question, Geoffrey's understanding (and mine) were greatly expanded.

Crediting also fosters independence by allowing children to draw their own conclusions about what they've done.

For example, to a child who has just sounded out p-a-t— pat, the teacher might say "you just read the word *pat.*"

This accomplishes two things. Describing the child's action—in this case putting those letter sounds together— gives the child confidence in his own ability and in the progress he is making. It also gives him the information that he has, in fact, read the word *pat.*

This allows children to make their own evaluation of the action undertaken. They can say to themselves: *Hmmmm. I must be pretty smart if I can read.* Thus, the child's satisfaction with himself or herself comes from within. In this way, children do not become dependent on outside sources for praise or good feelings. That is a major step in the formation of their self-esteem.

Personal Pronouns

Another important way to enhance children's individuality and importance is through the use of personal pronouns. In our language, first- and second-person pronouns carry a lot of weight; children are particularly susceptible to the use of "I" and "you." "David, your smile tells me that you are pleased with that painting." "Jane, I like the way you came down the stairs so quietly." There should be no doubt in Jane's mind what I think of her. Very pointedly, I direct my comments to her, about her actions. Credit is placed squarely on her accomplishments, not on my evaluation of her as a person. And I've "educated" her on a specific by giving her a descriptive ("quiet").

These pronouns carry so much weight that they can make children strong or diminish them in their own estimate. Children can bear the weight of correction if it is handled sensitively, or be crushed by it if it is not.

Perhaps Jackie pulls everything out from her mother's kitchen cabinets and the kitchen is a disaster. The mother's response is predictable. She yells, "Look what you've done. You're a bad girl!" Jackie hears, "you are bad."

Is this the image the mother wants Jackie to have of herself? What's more, Jackie gains a vivid mental picture of herself as a bad girl without a real understanding of what constitutes "bad." She has learned that pulling containers out from under the cabinet earns her mother's anger. But, if tomorrow she pulls everything out of her toy chest to find a special toy and doesn't earn her mother's anger, does she understand the difference? Does she know to replace the toys? Jackie's mother's response allows no opportunity for Jackie to learn from her experience or to apply the lesson to a similar situation. It only diminishes her opinion of herself, carefully reinforced by the use of the word *you*.

But let's look at a more sensitive approach Jackie's mother could have chosen. If she had said, "I am furious with what you've done. Put all the containers back in the cabinet," Jackie would have learned three things. One is that her mother disapproves of her action, another is the action necessary to correct her behavior, and the third is that she has not lost her mother's love as a result. Notice that the mother did not say, "I'm furious with you," but, "I am furious with what you've done." In this manner, Jackie's sense of being worthy of her mother's love is not threatened. Her self-esteem remains intact.

Concentration and cooperation in a multi-age classroom.

Descriptive Adjectives

The use of the word *bad* in this example illustrates the power of careful wording. Empty adjectives should be omitted. Words such as *wonderful, great, good, nice* — these don't carry a lot of meaning. When I tell you it's a "nice" day, you really don't know a great deal about the day. The sun may be shining without a cloud in the sky, or it may be hot, with a light breeze blowing. You don't know what "nice" means to me.

Jennifer brings a leaf to her mother and her mother says, "You found a pretty leaf!" Jennifer's mother is on the right track. She used the word *you* to give credit to Jennifer, and she used *found* as a descriptive verb. But what does "pretty" tell Jennifer about the leaf? What

71

makes the leaf "pretty"? If the leaf is pretty because it's autumn and the color is vivid, the mother could have said, "You found an orange leaf." Or, if the leaf is pretty because it's spring and the new leaf has veins through it, she could have said, "You found a leaf that shows its veins." Instead of "plastic" adjectives, use words with substance. Don't miss the opportunity to help your child learn to think descriptively.

Now, about the word *good*. Tell children that they are good and see what they will do. In *Between Parent and Child*, Haim Ginott says that they will immediately do something horrible because they are overwhelmed by the word *good*. Children feel that they can't possibly be "good" so they must do something that is "bad." An abstract term like *goodness* surpasses their ability to comprehend, so they must bring it to more manageable proportions. They know they can't live up to that expectation, so they manage it by proving you wrong. This is an important point to remember when you want your child to behave well, and it is certainly a graphic argument for using specific, understandable words when encouraging children.

Educating Words

Along with specific nouns and adjectives, it is important to use what I call "educating" verbs, like the verbs *to choose*, or *to discover*. These verbs expand children's understanding of their actions by giving those actions specific names. They may not understand them, but having performed the activity, they will grasp its meaning. These verbs give them a better working vocabulary.

I often hear parents say, "Do your shoes," instead of, "Tie your shoe laces." This may be a misguided attempt to use words the parent thinks the child understands, but the child is capable of discerning specific meanings in words. "Do" has become a multipurpose word that teaches a child nothing. This may stem from the parent being too tired to think of the correct word! But it's worth the effort. It is just as easy to say, "Clean your room," as, "Do your room." (And then we wonder why teenagers have such limited vocabularies!) Or, if parents say, "Do your calculations and your research," instead of, "Do your homework," maybe children would have a better idea of what they are supposed to be doing!

Paraphrasing

Another consideration in wording your responses to children and adults is borrowed from Synectics, developed by George Prince. In his book *The Practice of Creativity*, Prince cites the inability to listen as the major barrier to communication. Too often we try to evaluate what someone says to us rather than listen. We seem to fear listening. Consequently, the first requirement of communication is courage. Prince tells us to concentrate not on evaluating someone's idea, but on repeating it. To try and repeat someone's thought requires the listener's attention and the listener can't repeat those thoughts if his mind is racing ahead to evaluate the idea.

Prince's idea is to paraphrase. By listening to and repeating children's thought you gain two advantages. First, you let them know they are worthy of your attention and that they have been understood. And second, you set an example. By carefully listening and repeating, you help children learn how to listen and repeat. Through paraphrasing, children hear their own ideas reinforced by an adult and their sense of worthiness is enhanced. Paraphrasing is a helpful way to relate to young children whether you are a teacher, a parent, or a friend. Just give them back their words, and as you paraphrase you will have time to think about what they've said and to credit their thoughts and ideas. The reason little children repeat themselves so often is that they feel they are almost never heard.

Of course, paraphrasing can be abused. The nightmare I envision is that of a child going from teacher to teacher, and whatever they say is parroted back to them in a monotone.

Child: "I have a broken arm."

Teacher: "Oh, so you broke your arm."

This is clearly a gross exaggeration, yet the tendency is there. Paraphrasing can also become a way of avoiding genuine communication with the child.

Under the guise of remaining "nonjudgmental" it is also easy to assume a tone of voice which denies any emotion. Paraphrasing, then, must be seen as simply a tool to facilitate better interaction with children, not as a mechanistic formula for reacting. It will not be appropriate to every situation. If another approach seems more natural in some circumstances, parents or teachers should not feel bound to twist every response into a paraphrase. In this, as with so many of our communication strategies, we need to be flexible, to remember that "the letter of the law kills, but the spirit gives life."

Questioning

During my twenty years as a teacher, I noticed a strange thing about the way adults communicate with children: They ask the children questions constantly. I wondered why adults feel such an overwhelming need to pepper children with questions and finally decided it is because some adults are uncomfortable with children.

Even though many of the adults I had dealings with were parents, they appeared uncomfortable when talking with children and sought to hide this nervousness behind innocuous questions. Overtly, they would say they were asking questions to get to know the children better, but I felt that many questions were asked to keep the conversation going in a controlling way. Their nervousness didn't concern me as much as the damage they did in the process of questioning the children.

Our schools are steeped in the tradition of questioning and answering. I confess that when I first started teaching, it seemed to me that the teacher's job was to ask children the right questions. You were supposed to be giving them, on the one hand, the security of knowing the answers that they knew, and, on the other hand, the challenge of finding the answers they didn't know. On a more sophisticated level, you were leading them along that Socratic path to truth defined by a process of elimination. Reason would illuminate them and they would stand forth in its bright and pure light. I have since learned better.

Children a little older than our preschoolers know the fallacy of the questioning method. "If you've got the answer, what are you asking me for?" they might well ask. Hidden behind that is the idea that real questions have to do with things you're ignorant about, puzzled about, in real need of answers for. Something else is hidden there too: People learn what they need to learn and when they need to learn, not what and as someone else thinks they should learn. All growing is like that; it happens out of needs, which are unique, if generally predictable, in their sequence or their areas of concern. It's also organic, rising out of each person's relation to the people and things around and inside of him or her.

Question-and-answer teaching neglects the whole for a tiny part—perhaps an irrelevant part. More than that (and this is something children often remember with pain many years later), the method suggests that someone has a right to that part, thus to anything one knows or thinks—ultimately to anything private, quiet, secret, one's own. I could go on to state how it favors talkers

75

over doers, how it centers the attention on what the teacher wants rather than what the child is learning, how it encourages competition at the expense of cooperation, and so on. But let me sum it up: questioning is too often a violation of a child's wholeness and individuality.

You may remember the book of some years ago, *Where Did You Go? Out. What Did You Do? Nothing.* Those are the kinds of answers children learn to give, and parents and teachers all too often deserve them. Author and educator John Holt had some interesting things to say about this, too. He has written about how a child, desperate to satisfy a questioning teacher or parent, may give any answer at all, with the mad hope that it just might be "right."

Children are rigorously trained in guessing what is on the teacher's mind. When the guess is accurate they receive the reward, the teacher's lips forming that wonderful word RIGHT. The assumption that there is only one right answer, and that it is hidden somewhere in the teacher's brain cells, leads to the censoring of all other thoughts as irrelevant, immaterial, and just plain incorrect. The student learns to strategically outguess and outconnive the teacher and completely forgets that there is a problem worth being examined, analyzed, and responded to. This outguessing and outconniving inhibits, if not completely eliminates, the natural tendencies of speculating, analyzing, and answering in a way that is unencumbered by fears of outcome.

Obviously, I'm not saying that you never ask questions. You ask them when you need information a child can give you and may feel privileged and happy to give you. That's not testing; and testing is what I'm really unhappy about. Too many children's lives are punctuated with quizzes—with us adults as quizmasters. What I want to show you is that there are better ways to determine what children know than to set them up for failure by questioning them.

Again, it was John Holt who gave us the best rule of thumb for determining whether or not to ask a question. His rule is: "Never ask a child a question to which you already know the answer." According to George Prince, questions reject what another person is saying or may mask a hidden agenda. You can see this at work in the following example.

Cindy came home from school excited about a new material she had begun to work with. She was anxious to tell her mother all about it. When she came through the door, her mother automatically asked, "What did you learn in school today, honey?" And Cindy launched into her description of the Montessori red rods, telling her mother how they got smaller and how they fit together.

Cindy's mother began to question Cindy: "How many rods were there?" "Did Margaret show you how to put them together?" "When you put them together did they form a shape?" The hidden agenda at work here was the mother's determined effort to find out if Cindy had learned what her mother thought she should have learned.

Cindy told her mother what she had learned, but her mother rejected the idea that Cindy's "play" with the rods had taught her anything, because the mother already had in mind what she thought her daughter should have learned. And she proceeded to probe for the answers that she wanted. When Cindy couldn't answer her mother's questions, the mother "knew" that Cindy hadn't learned anything from this exercise. The mother had questioned to satisfy her own agenda, which was hidden from Cindy. Cindy didn't know what her mother was working toward.

Keeping in mind that children have amazing observation and learning abilities, look at what Cindy *did* learn through the question-and-answer exchange:

Cindy sensed, when she couldn't answer her mother's questions that she had failed in some way. She knew she had learned something new; in fact, she had learned such abstract concepts as visual discrimination and distinctions of various dimensions in long and short. And, if her mother had listened and demonstrated her listening ability by paraphrasing Cindy's words, she might have been able to determine that. Instead, her mother conveyed to Cindy that she had failed because she had not learned what her mother wanted her to learn. And Cindy *understood* that her mother rejected what she said. The damage to Cindy's self-esteem is bad enough, but in addition, she didn't go near the Montessori red rods for a long time.

No doubt, there will be times when you need to ask a child a question. But if it is for the sake of testing the child, the question is unfair. If the child doesn't answer as the adult wishes, there is a very real sense of having failed. You can probably recall a time when you raised your hand, eager to answer a question in school (believing that you knew the right answer), only to be told that you were wrong. The sense of devastation was complete. There will be many devastating moments in any child's life. I don't think we should add to them by asking needless questions for there are better ways of getting information from a child.

Better Ways of Getting Information

The way I like best is to say, "I'd like to know . . . your name!" With sincere interest behind those words, a child is happy to comply and feels genuinely appreciated. That one phrase can be used effectively in many cases. Cindy's mother could have said, "I'd like to know what you learned today" and then let Cindy tell her. Or she could have said, "I'd like to know what you think about that."

Another way to determine if a child knows something is to say, "Show me . . . how to tie your shoe," which lets a child demonstrate his knowledge. The point to remember here, however, is that you should only use this when you

Being at the child's eye-level is important to building self-esteem.

know that the child can tie his shoe or do what you wish to see performed. If the child is not able to show you how to tie his shoe, or do whatever was requested, you should respond by reaffirming what he was able to accomplish. "You showed me how to make a loop! That's the first step in tying a bow" (never missing that opportunity to help the child learn).

If you detect a common note in all of this, you're quite right. The underlying principle is one of support, of honoring a child's God-given ability, of regarding the child as a fully functioning, whole person. In a sense, I'm talking about the rights of children. But that's not the language I like to use—it too much implies the relationship of adversaries. Children's rights need defending from time to time, with all of the ammunition we can find, but I'm concerned here not with legal battles but with the finely woven fabric of everyday life—how we behave toward each other.

Body Language

As important as our words are, they can be reinforced or contradicted by our body language. So much has been said about body language, yet few people use the principles to their advantage. At CLC, the staff use specific gestures and movements to communicate with their children. The most obvious is getting down to the children's level. While teachers have bent over their students for years, this is not getting down to the children's level. What I mean is to get down, maybe on all fours, so that your eyes are on the same level as the child's. This means stooping, bending, and sometimes sprawling on the floor; and it can mean sore muscles too. But the children's sense of being on equal terms with their world is supported. The staff's respect for children is demonstrated every time a teacher sits on the floor and smiles encouragement directly into Suzy's face. Suzy can't help but know that she has earned the teacher's undivided attention and interest in what she has to say.

Another use of body language is in a teacher's finger movements when demonstrating a new learning material or concept. Using precise hand movements to emphasize the action we want the child to learn, helps the child visualize the idea. For instance, when I take the three-letter word board and sound out the three sounds, I use my thumb, index, and middle finger to represent each sound and then bring them together to emphasize the blending of the sounds. And it works.

Other uses of body language include smiling to show encouragement and pleasure—a long, loving hug or a quick squeeze to show affection and delight in a child's accomplishment—or perhaps stroking a child's hair to calm him or her. These expressive gestures may seem very natural, but too often they are withheld out of pre-occupation or anger. Children need the reassurance of physical gestures that boost their self-esteem.

Eye Contact

Another basic way in which we show respect for others is by establishing good eye contact. Not enough can be said for this simple idea. If you look directly into another adult's eyes when you speak to him, it is very difficult for his attention to wander. If you look directly into children's eyes, they are much more likely to concentrate on what you are saying and remember it than if you were to look elsewhere. Furthermore, they will learn to look directly at you when they are speaking. If you listen to them, looking them in the eye, you are much more likely to understand what they are saying than if you continue to wash the dishes or read while they talk. And they feel that their thoughts receive the attention they deserve. Campbell talks about correcting a child's serious behavior problem with "warm, pleasant, eye contact" (unconditional love) by the parents.

Tone of Voice

One last point needs to be addressed in our discussion of communicating with children: your tone of voice. The best rule of thumb to follow here is to speak to the child in the same tone of voice you would use with your best friend. If you would never dream of insulting your best friend by saying, "Lynn! Don't you look so-o-o swe-e-e-t in that pretty dress!" then don't use that drawn-out, sing-songy tone with a child.

And, if you tell your secretary, "I-want-you-to-type-a-letter-for-me," carefully enunciating each word and saying it slowly so that she is sure to understand, you will be very lucky to get that letter! Don't expect any better cooperation from your child if you use that slow approach.

Worse yet (and harder to demonstrate in writing) is that high, squeaky tone so many adults use with babies: "Goochee, goocheee, goo!" I'm convinced babies dislike that tone of voice as much as adults would if they were ever spoken to in that way.

The correct tone of voice to use with children is the one you use for adults, and at the same rate of speed. If you speak at a rapid rate, children will follow it just as easily as they will if you speak more slowly. The condescending tones of voice mentioned above relegate children to the rank of second-class citizens, with less than adult intelligence. I have walked down the hallways in schools and have heard teachers screeching at their children in those high, unnatural voices, only to have them turn when I entered the room and say in a normal voice, "Oh hello, Margaret." Why did they assume that the children would not respond to that same normal tone? Their intellectual ability is the same as an adult's, even if their scope of experience and accumulation of facts are not as vast.

As you've learned, solid communication skills make up a large part of the Children's Learning Center's communication style. All of the elements of communication, from precisely worded, descriptive feedback to the tone of voice used, are essential to building children's perceptions of themselves as worthy individuals. But we can convey this message to children in other ways, and not all are as elaborate or complex. We will look at one of the most important—environment—in the next chapter.

5

Environment

As you approach the Children's Learning Center you are greeted by a majestic row of evergreens. The school snuggles comfortably into the surrounding mounds of earth, the trees framing it almost storybook style. It is a one-story structure, somewhat large (about seventy-five feet across the front), yet apparently not intimidating even to the tiniest children. That is because of the illusion the architect created. In constructing the school, he had the land scooped out to allow the building to sit very low. Also, he positioned the school so that a hill had to be dug out on the east side, resulting in a two-foot embankment which edges that wall. The school looks small and cozy, nestled next to the embankment, with little hills, giant boulders, and towering fir trees in the play area all around it. Its appeal along with the sensation of discovery you feel when the curving driveway brings you suddenly upon it always makes me think of Snow White's delight when she happened upon the seven dwarfs' inviting little house.

When I first began plans for this building, I had a firm conviction that the design of a school and its furnishings should be intensely related to the learning process. That belief was strongly confirmed throughout my teaching experience—so much so that I cannot even talk about effective teaching without first dealing with the school environment.

The design of the school itself encourages a child to reach for something new. The school is carpeted to invite children to sprawl out while they read a book; it is designed without interior walls to tempt them to stretch a line of blocks as far as they want them to go, and it is decorated without clutter so as not to detract from the peace and harmony of working in an ordered environment. This idea of a spacious ordered learning center with well-thought-out materials is the essence of the Environment Strategy.

The classroom environment can stimulate children to learn or it can stifle them. CLC's environment does not intrude on the child's ability to assimilate information. The lines of the school are clean and precise, without fussy adornments. When children or adults enter the school, their interest is attracted by the materials displayed, not the room. And this is what we wanted to accomplish. Children can unconsciously absorb the environment as they move on to the learning materials with minds free to concentrate on the thinking process.

It was the unique design of our school building that first brought attention to CLC and our teaching methods.

The Educational Facilities Laboratories (EFL) of the Ford Foundation had earlier given us a $4,000 grant to aid in the planning stages. Upon the building's completion, the Laboratories praised it as "one of the few well-designed facilities for early childhood education in the United States," and described it as "free, open, warm, and intensively planned." Believing that the building should be better known, EFL granted us almost $21,000 to make a film that would show the school and explain the principles behind its design. Very soon, architects and educators were visiting us. And because the building is so related to our teaching methods, our program began to receive much attention as well. The school quickly evolved into a center where psychologists, materials specialists, and parents joined the architects and educators for study. This was a tremendous advantage for us, since these talented people had wonderful suggestions that strengthened and enhanced our program. My staff and I were always grateful for their contributions and we gave them much credit for the school's success.

The Unspoken "Message" of Structures

It is important to understand in planning a school that the building, the play area, the equipment, furnishings, and materials all communicate to the children. Their messages to them are usually the first ones the children receive each day and are perhaps the most pervasive throughout their time at school. With CLC's emphasis on self-esteem, we wanted our total environment to say to the child, "I respect you and I trust you!" We were fortunate in finding a talented architect who understood our needs, Egon Ali-Oglu of Cambridge, Massachusetts. He was interested in education and had already been experimenting with the communicative aspects of the classroom. He also developed the Componoform building system which suited our requirements and was extremely economical.

Excluding the cost of site preparation, our four thousand-square-foot, concrete schoolhouse cost only fourteen dollars a square foot when it was constructed in 1967.

The Componoform method consists of standard modular units—lightweight insulated wall sections and huge columns with four short horizontal crossbeams extending at right angles from the top. The units Egon designed were manufactured in New Jersey and then sent to Stamford where they were put in place by cranes. I found it fascinating to watch all the parts fit together so beautifully. It was as though the huge machines were working a giant puzzle.

Aside from the usual features that an effective building offers, this modular design offered a unique advantage to our students. Most children no longer have the chance to see how things are made. Normally, you don't see what is holding up a building or how it fits together. However, in this building, the structure is plain for all to see. The children can see the huge columns for the skeleton of the building. There are exposed beams holding up the high, pyramid-shaped roof in the center core area. The children can discern the separate roof slabs, walls, windows, and doors. They even learn the purpose of additional fixtures like gutter pipes by watching rainwater pour from them to a prepared rocky space on the ground. So the building speaks to the children and the learning process begins with the schoolhouse itself.

The Children's Learning Center is truly a joyful place —largely because of the freedom there. There are no classrooms where children can be lined up like parts in a factory. Instead, the building is filled with things like book gardens, sunken forums, and inside drawbridges. It is covered with a variety of textured, carpeted floors; there are light places, dark places, quiet places, loud ones. It's a place where there are textures to feel and music to hear, where food is set out to be always available, where experiments are to be made, and where the children can find things for matching and testing. There is a wood shop, a water place, and a sand place—one place distinguished by colors, others by shape. There are places where one can be alone. There are no bells, or periods, or grades. If this all sounds like Walt Disney World, the impression couldn't be more erroneous. Disney World is a place of unrepentant fantasy, which is fine in its place; CLC is the real world, scaled to the level of the child's comprehension ability.

The core of the Center is a large open space which accommodates six separate teaching orientations—math, science, language, art, music, and sensorial.

The core space allows children to develop self-esteem, to grow and acquire concrete skills. This is laced with low shelves, built with solid cinder blocks, six inches wide and four feet deep so they really are at the child's height. When a teacher stacks two or three of these upon a wooden board and then tops them with a freshly enameled pine shelf, they are still less than three feet in height.

The shelves are open so that the children can take material from either side. Another reason for this is that small children absorb information so readily that even when they are working in one section, they "tune" into what is being learned in another section. They aren't limited to learning just what is in front of them, but are receptive to everything going on around them.

Low Shelves and Dividing Walls

This is an environmental strategy that can easily be translated for use in a home or condo. Low shelves with pine boards and bricks can be built in your child's room. It's best not to position them flat against the wall but to angle them perpendicularly, for in that way the child can get at them from both sides; they also serve to break up the room's space. Plastering everything against the

Children love Forum time and can concentrate at very young ages.

wall and leaving a large open area in the middle of
the child's room invites him to spread his toys out. By
dividing the room with perpendicular shelves, you create
parts of it that invite work but also limit the space.

Environment

On the west end of CLC's interior is a Forum, an 8′ × 12′ sunken area with two rows of steps forming seats on all but one side. Here the children gather for songs, games, and stories. A one-way glass at the back of the Forum permits observation of the children from the large room behind. Called the CLC Institute, this 24 × 24-foot wing is for the faculty, visitors, and adult students.

Another wing, equal in size, is at the opposite end of the core room. This is the art area. There are large tables there for painting, sculpting with clay, and creating collages. An abundance of art materials is always available as well as hole punchers in profusion, tape, glue, string, yarn, and many materials that are recycled from the industrial world.

Near the center of this wing is a circular platform where juice and cookies are always available. A water-play table stands nearby. A nook at one end has tables and materials for practical-life activities. Only in the art area are there tables and a few chairs for the children. CLC long ago abandoned general use of the tables, desks, and chairs so characteristic of most nursery schools. They are too limiting and uncomfortable for the young child. The carpeting throughout the core area and north wing invites the children to sit or sprawl on the floor which is far more natural to them. In the home, is that not where most children play, read, and watch TV?

One of the ways CLC makes use of the environment to communicate with children is in the interior decoration, done in very neutral colors. The walls are white, the woodwork and ceiling beams are stained walnut brown, and the wall-to-wall carpeting is charcoal gray. This unobtrusive color scheme allows the children to stand out in the classroom.

The muted colors also accentuate the learning materials. The shelves are painted white and the supporting sections black. Children are attracted to brightly colored

89

A protected corner is created so that math can be easily learned.

materials. But a blue toy on a blue shelf is hardly noticed. Like jewelers, who display their diamonds against a backdrop of blue velvet, we ought to display our materials to each item's best advantage. When children enter the CLC room, their eyes go immediately to the brightly colored learning materials that stand out from the white shelves and gray carpet. And as staff members survey the room, the children become the most important visual attraction. My training in merchandising and art helped me to discover visual effects that worked for us.

Every few days the staff removes a few materials to make room for "new" items on the shelves. Rotating the learning materials works well to keep the children challenged and interested. This is what I call "merchandising" the materials.

I have found that my early retail career prepared me more than I knew for teaching, for to effectively motivate children you must display materials so that they "call out" to the children. The first thing to consider is that children are much smaller than you. Consequently, shelves, chairs, and tables need to be on the children's level. If learning materials are on a shelf beyond children's reach, where they cannot see them, it isn't likely that they will be motivated to work with those materials. This is a simple idea, yet we show tremendous respect for children when we consider the world from their perspective.

Retailers have been considering children from this angle for years. In most grocery stores, you will notice a toy section for babies and children. The baby toys will be hung on a rack at an adult's shoulder level. Since most small children are seated in a shopping cart, those toys are exactly on the child's eye level. Older children who are free to walk beside the cart will be attracted by the more sophisticated toys, placed at an adult's hip level or lower, within eye-catching reach of your child. If this idea can be used effectively to sell toys, it can also be used to help your children reach those materials that will teach them.

The Strategic Use of Space

Of more importance than the contrast in colors in a room is the use of space. If many children's toys are crowded together on shelves, where they can't be distinguished from each other, they lose their individuality. If we clear the space surrounding an item, the material has a greater impact on the children. In addition to this, children will note the exact position of that material on the shelf and return it to its assigned location. Like information stored in a computer, that learning material has a specific address to the children and their sense of order will insure that it can always be found in that location.

The number of toys displayed in many preschools for children virtually overwhelm them. Only a limited number of items should be available for the child to choose each day. At CLC, only a fourth of the learning tools are in the school at one time. The remaining three fourths are kept in storage and brought out only to replace an item, when that item has been used repeatedly and the children no longer are attracted to it.

This is a good practice to follow with your children's toys at home as well. I suggest you keep two-thirds of them on high shelves. If you feel that your child has grown disinterested with a particular toy, ask him or her if something else is preferred, or just unobtrusively replace that one. You'll quickly find out if the child misses that toy. If children want another toy off the shelf, let them decide what they want to put away.

All of this amounts to giving children and their possessions the respect you expect them to give you, and your things. If you consider the things you value in your home, you will realize that you display them to their best advantage, attractively and prominently so that others will notice them. For instance, you might place a lovely vase on a favorite antique cabinet where it may be reflected in a mirror and on adult eye level. You may remove everything else on the cabinet to set the vase off. If you place flowers in the vase to complement it, you present it in an even more favorable light. I feel that a child's valuable possessions ought to be given the same treatment.

This care for the children's materials is just one more way that we communicate respect to the child. I'm sure parents do not realize that they seem to be devaluing children's property when they give them a big toy box in which to throw their toys. If you can, provide shelves for their playthings, no matter how inexpensive they are. Treat their cheapest plastic toy—in the way you pick it, the way you hold it, and how you place it carefully on the shelf—as if it were a piece of crystal. The respect you have shown their toys will register as respect for them, and it will mean more than you may imagine. After that, you may find them showing more care for your things.

I want to add another word about toys. Invest in quality toys for your children. It's better to give them fewer materials of higher quality than an abundance of cheap plastic toys that will fall apart the third time they are used.

Basic Materials for the Child

Many excellent didactic materials are available for children today, but you don't have to spend a fortune to provide quality learning materials for your child. Some of the oldest, most basic toys are best for encouraging a child's creative thinking. If your funds are limited I would suggest the following starter materials:

1. *Picture Books*

Choose books that are easy to handle and to read. Look for color, too. Think how much more quickly you are drawn to a child's book in the library that contains detailed, beautifully colored illustrations, than the usual variety of books for children you see on the shelves of many stores.

Avoid purchasing children's books that have unclear lettering. Fancy lettering, for example, is harder for children to read and they won't recognize the letters as easily when they are trying to learn the alphabet. A good kind of print is simple and round. Even better, though maybe harder to find, are books written with all capital letters.

I cannot emphasize enough the importance of exposing young children to the written word. The beauty of words is so key to molding the soul of a child. I feel strongly that parents should read to their children every night, and not just the little "grocery store" books. There are many wonderful classics for children of every age.

Some of the best feedback I received over the years from parents came as a result of the books I read during Forum time. I always held the book out so that its open pages were facing the children, and moved it around so they could see it while I read "upside down." One mother reported peeking into her daughter's room one afternoon and seeing her sitting with her dolls arranged around her like in the Forum. She was holding a book upside down and "reading" to them, repeating every word from the story verbatim. Children do have wonderful memories. After you have read a story to them several times, they will often be able to repeat every word exactly (sometimes even adding appropriate sound effects). Their pride in their ability to "read" this way will stimulate a lifelong interest in books.

2. *Puzzles*

Puzzles are an obvious—and delightful—way to develop young children's minds as they learn to identify shapes and sizes. Puzzles encourage them to develop memory skills also, and placing the shapes in exact spaces develops manual coordination. Try to find the wooden puzzles that have a knob on each piece. This way, children won't get in the habit of turning the completed puzzle over and simply dumping the pieces on the floor. Knobs encourage children to remove each piece, one by one. This is one of those subtle messages that teaches children so much about order and respect for property.

3. *Standard Kindergarten Blocks*

Blocks of all shapes and sizes are a proven tool for helping children build, create, invent, and challenge themselves. Nothing is "given" to children when they take a collection of blocks and go to work. There are no power motors to make things go, move, or perform.

Concrete learning materials help children to understand place value (math).

When you purchase blocks, buy as many as you think your home can comfortably handle. Children delight in stretching their creations in a seemingly endless train across an entire room, or reaching for the ceiling. It gives children great joy to accomplish so large a feat. Every time the blocks stretch farther or climb higher, it stretches their perception of possibilities. So, if possible, allow them to explore big, to build big, to think big, wonderful thoughts about themselves as they pioneer with their hands and their minds.

4. *Tempera Paint*

I'll talk more about painting later, but it's important that children have regular opportunities to express themselves with paints and crayons. Tempera paint is relatively inexpensive and can be purchased at any art store, in liquid or powdered form. I'll also offer some tips later on ways to keep the artistic mess to a minimum.

I feel strongly that one of the most important ways we can show our respect for children is to provide for them the same kind of orderly environment which we appreciate. I know it is fashionable today to assume that children's bedrooms and classrooms must be filled with colorful clutter, but I think that is just another way in which we patronize children. I have discovered that they respond to aesthetically pleasing colors and designs just as we do. Perhaps two examples will illustrate my point.

A Sense of Order

Suppose your best friend, Lynn, is coming from Dallas to visit you for a week. You want everything to be clean and perfect for her so you scrub and wax the house so that it gleams. The guest bedroom is given special attention. You might even purchase a new bedspread and curtains to brighten it up. If not, at least the bedspread and curtains are freshly laundered. Clean sheets are put on the bed. Being a thoughtful hostess, you might put candied mints in a dish and arrange fresh flowers in a vase on the bedside table. All the little extra clutter that had found its way into the guest bedroom is removed and stored in some other closet. Everything is neat and in order.

Now let's peek into your child's room across the hall. Bright curtains and bedspread let you know immediately that this is a child's room. Sneakers are carelessly tossed in the corner. Shelves line an entire wall and are packed with your child's favorite things. His books are there, his stuffed animals are there, and his favorite baseball team's pictures are taped to the walls. Under his bed is the box with his electric train set. On top of his dresser is his baseball glove and baseball, along with a lamp made from a football helmet. In the corner of the room, the toy chest is filled with games, toy soldiers, trucks, cars, etc. On the back of the door is a set of hooks that hold his jacket, his robe, and pajamas. And beneath the shelves are his desk and chair, and another lamp. The top of the desk is covered with his drawings; the drawers are filled with crayons, pencils, paper, paper clips, ruler, and scissors. This is a typical boy's room—ordered chaos. No fresh flowers in here; there isn't any room!

For some reason, adults believe that children naturally exist in a state of structured pandemonium and can only feel secure when surrounded by an excess of familiar items. The converse does not hold true, however, for adults. As adults, most of us insist on the simple, uncluttered environment which frees our minds and lets us think.

The fact is, children require the same sense of order as adults, and may require it to an even greater degree. In *The Absorbent Mind*, Montessori presented a child's need for order and, in essence, maintained that what a child sees and hears at the earliest age is "incarnated" by the child. As adults we might remember the layout of a room, but the child internalizes it. This internalization becomes fixed in children's minds and remains with them throughout their lives. Their sense of order and balance is determined by this early introduction to their environment. If they are forced to adapt to an environment that is contrary to their fixed picture, the disharmony interferes with their ability to process into logical thought what their senses tell them.

As both parents and teachers we must rid ourselves of the assumption that children have to be messy. We need to change our expectations from the time that they are babies onward. We should not expect them to be childish, but expect them to be children of God and give them opportunities to express the natural sense of order he has placed within them. Don't allow your baby's room to be disorderly. Babies are constantly learning, visually and sensorially, from you and from the environment you provide for them. So set up an orderly room. Don't expect them to toss their toys around; but when they do, don't be angry. That will cause rebellion, even in a baby. Instead, pick up the toy and say, "This goes here."

Babies are going to experiment. They are also fascinated with dropping things from the high-chair tray. That's another way of learning. Don't get upset at babies because they mess food around or drop things; that's how they learn cause and effect. Instead, teach them. Say, "It fell three feet." We don't need to become angry with children because they are learning. We need to love them and teach them which ways of learning are appropriate and which are not. Instead of turning mealtimes into battles, let them be growing experiences.

Give your child every opportunity in a loving way to have an orderly room. As soon as a baby is able to get out of its crib, it can be put on a mattress on the floor. A fitted sheet and a comforter can double as a top sheet and blanket, so that a young child can learn to make its bed early. I know of some very young children who like to lie in bed, pull the comforter up, and slip out, as in a sleeping bag.

I see so many parents hassling their children because they scatter pieces of toys around or because they fling their coat down when they come in the door. But when I look at these children's homes, I can see that the parents have done nothing to make it easier for the children to be neat. At home there are no low shelves, or low hooks for them to hang their clothes on. We have easy access to our closet; why shouldn't our children?

If you have several children, assign to each one a colored hook (let them pick out the color), and a plastic dish pan or small laundry basket of the same color. Teach them to put coats, mittens, hats, and boots in the dish or basket, or on the hook as soon as they take them off.

Environment

Then, anytime one of those items is found outside these designated places, you have reason to complain. Giving each child his or her own color-coded bin and hook also helps eliminate the familiar lament, "Bobby's wearing my gloves," or "Suzy lost my hat."

When children are very young, you may want to color-code their toys also. Put a tiny piece of red tape on a toy and another piece on the toy shelf. This is an excellent learning technique, teaching children to match red to red, and it also helps them remember the location of the toy's home. If you give young children complicated toys that have lots of pieces, take time to color-code each piece so that the children know all the pieces of the same color belong to one toy.

Young children like to be near their parents. When you are cooking in the kitchen, your child is not going to want to be in the playroom, no matter how gorgeous or well-ordered it is. The facts of life are that he is going to want to be with you. To make it possible for you to get some work done, give him some work to do also. Keep a collage box—one of those small, multi-drawered cardboard chests—in the kitchen. Put crayons, markers, and scissors in it, and label it with the child's name. If you have several children, each child should have at least a shoebox in the kitchen that has something in it for him to do, so that he can do his work while Mom does hers. Children need to feel that each room has a spot for them. If you have a formal living room, you may want to make that room off-limits; but don't bar the children from it totally or they will humiliate you when a guest comes and explore it as if it were a new planet!

Another word about visitors. Children want to be around adults, not just their parents. So when Aunt Susie comes to visit, the children want to be able to play in the same room where she is. They want to be able to listen to what the adults are saying and watch what they are doing,

99

but they are going to be bored if they have to sit up straight on the sofa in their Mary Jane shoes and party dresses the entire afternoon. What you have to do as an adult is provide them an environment in which they can absorb their culture—the culture of how you interact with Aunt Susie. Give them something they can do quietly, in comfortable clothes, in a corner of the room where your visitor is sitting.

All of these techniques are really centered on love. The way you place the shelves, the way you think through the problems young children may encounter in accomplishing any task, the time and effort you take to create a comfortable learning environment for your children; all of this spells love, and respect.

Learning Through Art

A focal point in the CLC core area is a striking 4' × 4' painting of black and white geometric designs. It has the distinction of being chosen for a special showing in the Whitney Museum of American Art in New York City. The artist, Norman Ives, visited CLC and was so impressed with the variety and quality of art experiences we were offering our pupils that he donated the painting to the school. We felt highly honored and were thrilled with the gift because the painting seemed as though it were made for the decor. The children have always been fascinated by it and have never marked on it nor defaced it in any way. Their response to such fine art strengthens my belief that children should have beautiful art to enjoy— not just the popular contemporary pictures and posters made for children.

I feel passionately about the need to give children frequent art opportunities, for it is one of the best ways to encourage creativity in them. With some careful thought and planning you can create an art area in your home.

A drawing table or a hollow core door laid flat makes a

large, expansive space for children. Many artists have agreed that children should not paint on easels because the force of gravity tends to cause such paintings to be full of long, vertical lines. The edge of the easel limits a child's horizons. You want to give them large, flat spaces on which to paint.

You can make life easier for yourself by putting down some heavy plastic wrap like the kind used for storm windows. Tape it down with duct tape to the floor and then place cinder blocks on top, laying the door on these.

I recommend using tempera paints, rather than water colors, for tempera has more body; the water colors are disappointing to young children because the colors they make are frequently too washed out and thin. Put the paint in heavy-duty, thick, glass containers—furniture coasters work well. In this way, the container is less likely to turn over.

We learned to dilute the paints and found that the colors remained just as rich. Mixing them with half tempera and half liquid soap not only makes the paints go farther; it helps make the spillage easier to wash out.

Muffin tins or glass coasters on cookie sheets become palettes with red, yellow, and blue and can be made stable by taping them to the door. You want to eliminate the kind of things that make childhood messes, not because children necessarily mean to make a mess, but because they are not as thoughtful or as coordinated as adults.

Buy some sturdy, large brushes that won't shed their bristles immediately. You can find them in stores that carry Asian import materials. Another suggestion is to limit the source of water the children can use. Children have no sense of how far water is going to spill.

Allow children to mess around with paint. They love to experiment with mixing colors, but be prepared; they always overmix at first and end up with muddy, gray-brown

Children love the process of art and often don't really care about the product.

colors. Don't be worried that their black and brown hues signal some deep psychological problem. Children are not concerned with the final product. They're not creating something to look good on the refrigerator. They are interested in the process.

When you're commenting on your children's art, say things like, "You really concentrated for a long time on that painting. I like the way you put red next to blue." Don't try to guess what the painting "is" or portrays. Don't take your adult's imagination and try to impose it on the child, or try to make a "house" look like a house, or a "flower" look like a flower. Give them pluses about what you enjoy about their painting. And if you really hate it because it's just one big brown blob, say with love, "You know you spent twenty minutes on that; you're really enjoying your work!" and let it go at that. Don't try to be an art critic. Just give them loving feedback. Love is what makes your home what it ought to be.

Music, Too, Has Its Place

At CLC we found that our students also appreciated fine music as well as fine art. In the art area, classical music plays softly all morning—Bach, Vivaldi, Scarlatti—and the children love it. I feel that we do not need to withhold so much from children until they are "ready." You can begin to unlock meaning for your children from their earliest months. It doesn't matter how young they are, as long as you are not expecting a certain response or asking questions and expecting answers to come right back. You can simply say, "That's Beethoven you're listening to." They may not understand that, but you'll be surprised that when they are older they can identify some of the masters because you said, "Vivaldi always plays in this manner," or "Bach plays in that style."

I heard a wonderful story recently which confirms my theory that children absorb information that is far beyond their level of conscious understanding. A well-known conductor had been invited to participate in a benefit concert in a distant city. Due to a very tight schedule, he did not receive the music that was to be performed until he arrived for rehearsals. As he began to study it, he found that one of the pieces was new to him. He had never conducted it before. However, when he started rehearsing with the orchestra, he found, to his surprise, that he knew every bar and anticipated every movement. Several weeks after the concert, in a conversation with his mother, he happened to mention this puzzling occurrence. "That doesn't surprise me a bit," she exclaimed. "You must have heard that piece two hundred times. I played it constantly throughout my pregnancy."

Another area in which I think we often underestimate children's ability to understand is in the spiritual realm. I don't like the treatment that most children get in church nurseries. Too often it is patronizing, and it subtly implies that a child is less of a creature of God than an adult. I think it is much better for children to attend church with their parents than for them to be left in most church nurseries I've seen. If parents will give it a little thought ahead of time, the church worship hour doesn't have to be a trying experience. I recommend that the parents take with them to worship a small box of things that the children can quietly play with. Before that, I suggest a clear, serious talk with the children before the family enters the service. Let them know that this is a place where they have to be quiet. As children are coloring on a blank piece of paper they will take in more than we imagine of the ritual, the richness of the service, and even the words the pastor is preaching so eloquently from the pulpit.

As parents, you have limitless opportunities to teach your children if you see those opportunities as your God-given potential and if you realize that anyplace can be a learning place—your home, school, church, even your backyard.

Natural Play Areas

At CLC, the playground outside is considered another classroom. The entire area surrounding the school is available to the children. It is enclosed by a split-rail fence to which is nailed wire, netlike fencing. There is much of interest to explore there, because the grounds have been kept as natural as possible. Most playgrounds, parks, and lawns are leveled and cleared to the point that many children no longer experience nature in its virgin state.

Since CLC's land was cultivated back in colonial days, it offers the children natural wonders in the vast size of its trees and bushes, and in its beauty. Egon thoughtfully had huge boulders planted in the yard in such a way that they nestle together and create good body-building and climbing experiences. The two-foot embankment at one side of the building is a popular place for jumping, and another favorite spot is the large sand area we made nearby.

We planted in the playground some large, old forsythia bushes that grew sheltering tentacles which were just right for the children. They weren't hurtful or sticky. In the way they branched over they allowed the children to create rooms or apartments under them which they did with delight. We almost never went into the forsythia bushes, but the children played busily there. We also had a large mulberry bush with wonderful tasting mulberries from which we made jams every summer. In the front of the school there was an old apple orchard. One year, the children and teachers went straight through the Betty Crocker cookbook for children and made every apple recipe it contained.

We planted as many different kinds of trees as we could—cedars, bamboo, pine, and others—so the children could experience a variety of textures and smells. We also tried to vary the textures on the ground, using wood chips, sand, and different types of grass.

An added advantage of CLC's location is that it is directly across the street from the Stamford Museum and Nature Center, which is home for a variety of farm animals as well as more exotic types. We always took the children over in the spring to watch the baby calves, lambs, pigs, and ducklings being born.

In back of the school is a spacious area for running and for games; it's a lovely, one-acre meadow fringed by maple, oak, and dogwood trees. In this space is the only playground equipment we wanted to allow. A large dome is there, made of wooden two-by-fours at wide enough intervals for climbing, with a rope swing hanging from its center, and soft hay on the ground underneath. A tire swing hangs from a tree nearby. We didn't want the usual type of swings, because they too frequently cause accidents. The children don't seem to notice our lack of traditional playground equipment. We have taken advantage of the natural assets of the land to give them old-fashioned, creative opportunities for outdoor play.

As you can see, there is nothing haphazard about the environment of the Children's Learning Center—inside or out. We have taken seriously Montessori's belief that "a child can only develop fully by means of experience in his environment." We have planned our environment very carefully to support the learning process—wherever it takes place.

6

Roles

At the Children's Learning Center we developed a technique to help us meet the needs of each child, much as his or her parents would. The technique is called "Roles." And while no teacher, regardless of how dedicated, can ever be an entirely satisfactory substitute for a loving parent, the method does provide an excellent form of extended parenting. In its most basic terms, each adult at CLC is assigned a specific role each day. The roles are Head Teacher, Greeter, Rover, Coach and Video Coach.

Greeter and Rover

One of the things that bothered me the most when I was looking at schools for David was the chaotic way they

107

started their day. Parents—usually mothers—would go to the door with their children, and while a staff member would come to chat with thém, nobody paid attention to the children. When the mothers tried to leave, the children clung to their skirts and cried. There was anarchy for the first hour of school and that seemed to set the tone for the rest of the day.

At CLC, tearful separations are avoided by designating one staff member each day as the Greeter. Greeters meet the children at the car. They smile and extend a hand or give a hug to each child, making him or her feel welcome and wanted. Greeters, by opening the car doors, also allow children to leave their parents, rather than the parents leaving the children. It's much easier for children to leave their mothers, than vice versa. This small action reinforces their sense of self and independence; they are persons in their own right and can venture forth away from their parents on their own initiative.

After all the children have arrived, the Greeter assumes the role of a teacher for the rest of the morning. When it is time for the children to go home, the Greeter once again helps the children find their coats and makes sure that everyone is escorted to the right carpool.

Once the children are inside the school, the Rover takes responsibility for helping them. Throughout the day, the Rover provides protection for the children and the staff. Protection? Yes, protection. The whole purpose of roles is to segregate responsibilities so that each staff member is free to devote full attention to the assigned task.

There is no confusion or overlap of boundaries. So that the Head Teacher is free to teach without interruption, the Rover provides all the hugs and kisses for skinned knees. The Rover helps mop up the spills and accidents that are going to happen simply because children are children, without perfect eye-hand coordination yet.

The Greeter begins the day with a genuine welcome.

Additionally, the Rover wears a red arm band so that the children know whom to go to for the one-to-one attention they would receive if they were at home with their parents. The Rover is the one to whom they go if they need a Band-aid or dry pants, or art material that isn't available, or a coat buttoned, or if they have a problem. If a child climbs too far up a tree, the Rover's job is to help him get down.

One of the biggest advantages of this is that Rovers know their role and expect to take care of details that day. If, for example, one of the teachers, Brian, is working with a child and hears an argument start, he doesn't lose eye contact with that child or quit working to see what is happening. That's a way of respecting the child he is working with and maintaining a peaceful tone in the classroom. On the other hand, if a teacher is one of the Rovers for the day, he'll usually start a lesson with a child by saying, "I'm the Rover and I may have to be interrupted." That tells the child, "it's not that I don't care about you, but I have this job to do."

Another advantage to this system is that the Rovers are receptive when a child wants to show them a treasure; that's their function for the day. Thus the adult is not annoyed but receptive to the child. A Rover can bend down to a child's eye level, peering at a tiny bug in the palm of the child's hand and say with all sincerity, "That's an ant you have in your hand. I bet it tickles when it crawls up your arm."

It is also the function of the Rover to handle discipline. In most cases, stating one of four simple rules is sufficient: "People are not for hitting," or "running is for outside," or "put your work away so another child can use it," or "juice and crackers stay at the juice and cracker table." The rules are simple, easily visualized axioms that children understand. The difference is in the delivery. An angry parent might shout, "Stop running right now!" causing the child to lower his head and have his feelings hurt. When the Rover states calmly, "Running is for outside," the children don't feel put down.

Head Teacher and Teachers

Of course, the purpose of all the roles is to facilitate teaching and everyone, except for the Video Coach, teaches everyday. The Head Teacher administratively runs the school for the day. His or her primary responsibility is to make certain that the children receive the lesson planned for them that day. The Head Teacher also conducts large-group activities such as exercise, storytelling, and singing, and may assign staff members other roles, such as asking an In-depth Teacher to put on a Rover band for a period of time. Although the Head Teacher is in charge of classroom management for that day, nobody "supervises." Every staff member sits on the floor with the children, teaching or watching. I requested that teachers would take time to simply observe, and I always told new teachers, "You don't have to look busy." There are lots of photos of me sitting on the floor just "doing nothing." Of course, in five minutes a child would crawl up in my lap and end my rumination.

At the end of the morning, the Head Teacher leads everyone in a brief exercise period, and then conducts the morning's final group activity in the sunken Forum area. This can be finger games, a sing-along or—one of our most popular activities—an affirmation chart.

The affirmation chart, which we do on birthdays, has special meaning for children. If it is Johnny's birthday, the teacher writes, "Happy Birthday, Johnny!" on a huge sheet of brown paper. She then places it on the floor for Johnny to lie on while she traces the outline of his body with a colored marker. Next, she hangs the paper on the wall in front of all the children. This simple action has tremendous importance for children. For young children, the body is what they know of themselves. They relate strongly to size. And when you draw around their body with a magic marker, you enhance that size. The traced outline also catches a child's characteristic physical mannerisms. Children can look at the image and say, "Yes, that's just how Connie tilts her head." So these crude drawings often capture the essence of a child at three. Putting the outline on a large piece of butcher paper and hanging it up, emphasizes the child's importance.

Once the drawing is in place, the children tell Johnny what they like about him, while the teacher writes their comments on the chart. The remarks are sincere and often touching:

"I like the way he eats crackers with me . . . "
"His eyes sparkle . . . "
"He waits for me . . . "
"I like his smile."

One of the most important things about the affirmation chart is that the adult is recording exactly what each child says, without interpretation or comment. In an adult's mind, saying that someone eats crackers with you doesn't seem to be affirming anything. But the child who hears it understands the inference, that, to put it in adult psychological terms, "he cared enough about me to spend time over something simple like eating crackers."

I frequently hear adults in day-care centers taking some childish statement of friendship or affirmation and rephrasing it in more "acceptable" (adult) language. The key to the affirmation chart is that it is totally generated by the children. Afterward, Johnny gets to take the chart

At birthdays, an "affirmation chart" gives children opportunity to say: "I like the way you smile at me."

home and hang it on his bedroom wall. Some children tell me that they leave the chart up for a whole year, so they really do cherish that affirmation.

Affirmation charts are also beautiful things to do at a family birthday party. And I recommend not limiting it to the children. When it's Mother's or Daddy's birthday, do an affirmation chart for each one. Nothing is funnier to children than having Daddy lie down and tracing around him. And nothing is more touching than having the children tell Daddy what they love about him.

All of the CLC teachers are called "In-depth Teachers" because their time is concentrated primarily on teaching each child his or her planned lesson. They work hard at making children feel important just by the way they invite them to a lesson. If I wanted to do a math lesson with Martha using the unifix cubes I might approach her and say, "I saw you last week working with the cubes and I'd like to work with you again on that. You seemed to be really learning a lot from that." If she resisted, I would never insist. I would respect the fact that, in their child-time understanding, children may indeed have some really important tasks in mind.

I feel that learning happens best when a child has truly agreed to come to the lesson. So if I approached Martha and she said she had something else on her mind, my words would be, "Let's make a contract for later." We posted such contracts behind their pictures on a contract board, which also increased their self-esteem because they enjoyed touching their pictures on the board and seeing each other's names posted below the pictures. This became a kind of meeting place in the classroom.

Bruno Bettelheim explains just how important it is that we respect a child's "work."

What happens when a child is engrossed in play and the parents are ready to go out? They call him to come and get dressed. Or perhaps they want him to greet a visitor, or come to the table for lunch. His answer is, as ours would be in an analogous situation, "Not now—I'm busy." Are we prepared to honor our child's statement, as we expect him to honor ours? Or do we insist: "You come here, right now?" If we do, then we have once again succeeded in impressing on him that we do not take his activities as seriously as we do our own. Worse, we have demonstrated that we do not take his activities seriously at all when they conflict with our plans. If we truly took our child's play as seriously as we take our own tasks, we would be as loath to interrupt it as we are reluctant to be interfered with when we are working. This is the pattern demanded by consistency and a sense of fairness.*

We found that the children responded well to the role system. They seemed to delight in understanding the various roles. In addition, we were teaching them that some things are appropriate for some people at some time. They learned whom to interrupt—not to run to just any adult when they had a need.

Coaches

Everyday, someone is assigned the role of Pad-and-Pencil Coach. The Pad-and-Pencil Coaches teach, but they also schedule their time so that they can coach three staff members during the day. They sit beside the teacher, watching and listening, and record what they see and hear. During the staff meeting, they present their findings for their co-workers in the form of three pluses and a wish.

The three pluses they offer give all the staff members the chance to learn from each other. For example, the Coach might note in his pluses that first, the teacher was choosing her words carefully, responding to what was happening with the child at the moment; there was nothing stereotyped in her response. Second, the Coach might praise the teacher for keeping her hands in her lap and not reaching out to correct or straighten. Often when children are doing a lesson which requires lining up blocks or cubes or placing letters on something, they will line them up a little crookedly. They do not have the coordination or spatial perception to do it perfectly. At such times it's often difficult for teachers to resist the impulse to put everything into perfect alignment, so this plus was a reward for the teacher for keeping her hands

---

* Bruno Bettelheim, "The Importance of Play," *Atlantic Monthly* 251, March 1987, p. 35.

Pad-and-pencil coaching happens every day.

to herself when the Coach knew she would rather have straightened things up.

The last plus might be that the teacher didn't look up when there was a loud cry from the art area. She was not the Rover and she didn't allow herself to be distracted. She stayed "in character" as an In-depth Teacher.

The wish might be that since the child was responding so well to the lesson, the teacher might have worked with her another ten minutes, expanding the boundaries of her learning time. The wish is given and received as a chance to grow, not a criticism.

The Video Coach does not teach during the day. The staff members, when assigned this role, are given responsibility for taping the children and the teachers as they work together. They research small segments of videotape to be shared at the staff meeting, choosing segments that will offer opportunities for the rest of the staff

116

to comment on positive points. The Video Coach expresses one wish. I will say more about this role in the next chapter.

I modeled our system of roles on the system used by the Leicestershire schools. Those schools were unique in their treatment of children and faculty. The headmaster of the school was autonomous, governing his realm of teachers, aids, and students with equal consideration and respect. There was no sense of hierarchical pretension, but rather a serious devotion to helping children learn.

The adults willingly accepted specific responsibilities as aids or teachers. And the children recognized the function of the various adults. I was concerned that a caste system might develop among the teacher, director, and the aids and, after implementing the rotation strategy, was pleased to see that it was a good idea. By means of the rotation of roles, the staff kept in touch with the children; this helped us not lose sight of our purpose.

With this method of daily role rotation, no one staff member becomes just an intern or a supervisor of the playground, removed from the learning process. Instead, everyone shares these responsibilities. It doesn't matter if you are an eighteen-year-old intern; when it is your turn to be Head Teacher, everyone respects the fact that you are in charge. If you are a very rigid person you might appoint more Rovers; that is your decision and the school's director does what you say. Even when I was the head of the school, I never jumped in and took over. Of course, if the Head Teacher asked for advice I was glad to give it, but I tried to get rid of that situation that so often exists between principals and teachers in which there isn't much respect for the teacher.

Rotating roles also provides everyone with fresh

ideas, as a student-teacher might assume the role of Head Teacher and contribute a new insight through her eagerness. This keeps the staff from becoming stale, and it also keeps them humble. Each teacher has the opportunity of being Head Teacher and they all also have the privilege of being Mother Teresas for a day, dealing with smelly diapers, dirty socks, etc. After you've spent some time in the bathroom with a child you think, "Oh, Lord, is this really what I'm supposed to be doing?" And then you say, "Yes, it is. A child is experiencing my gentleness so he or she can learn to be gentle."

Roles Are for the Family, Too

Although I'm talking primarily about how these ideas work in a classroom situation, I feel strongly that they can and should be transplanted to the family. I often suggest that parents take roles on weekends, so that one parent will be free to do his or her work protected by the other parent who is taking care of the minute-to-minute needs of the children. If Dad is the designated Rover for Saturday morning, the children know not to run to Mom if a knee gets skinned or if they want permission to go to the movies with their friends.

Also, if one parent usually handles certain activities, it is good to switch around. Let Dad take the girls to ballet practice or all the children to church. If you observe families in church, 90 percent of the time—if only one parent is there—it will be the mother. If both parents are there, the mother will almost always be the one paying attention to the children. Switching roles increases children's chances of really experiencing their parents as whole persons who understand their interaction in a variety of roles, not always as the worrier, the disciplinarian, the sentimentalist, or the drill master. It also helps parents to see their children from different perspectives.

If you are in a teaching situation in which you have two

or more teachers, I heartily recommend this aspect of dividing roles to maintain discipline in the classroom—with the role of Rover a rotating role, so that each member of the classroom team is experienced by the children as a total person and not always in the role of "no sayer." If there is a job hierarchy, I recommend that the teachers give that up and exchange roles in an egalitarian way with one another so that the changing of the roles will allow each person on staff to understand the children more completely. The Head Teacher can thus see a totally different picture of her classroom activity and of her children's personalities by taking on what may be called in some schools an aid's role. She will see that being a good Rover calls for enormous talent and ability. The role of Rover is one of the keys to good classroom management, or what makes "good discipline" happen.

Having the Rover clearly identified as the disciplinarian is another way of respecting children. Children are children. The Bible is right—their heart is "full of foolishness." If a friend is at the other end of the room and a boy wants to talk to him he will go tearing down the middle of the room to reach him. Instead of ten teachers saying "don't!" one Rover will go quietly to the child and say "running is for outside."

The most common comment I got from people who observed the school was how peaceful the children looked. Their bodies were relaxed, their shoulders were relaxed, their faces were relaxed. Part of the reason, I think, is that they knew they weren't going to be put down. There was no need to be defensive. They knew that if they kept running, somebody was going to take their privilege away. They'd lose their freedom, which was held out as their great gift from the adult.

Whether you are establishing discipline in the classroom or in your family, two of the most important keys are simplicity and consistency. We burden children with

119

too many rules, demanding too much too soon. I think this is especially true in the area of manners. We try too hard to train young children to have good manners. We are constantly telling them, "Say, please, and thank you," or asking accusingly "why didn't you speak to Mrs. Brown when she was here?" Even worse, after a childish shoving match, we force the guilty parties to apologize. I never ask a young child to say he's sorry for hitting another child. It's impossible for preschool children to feel genuine sorrow or penitence. They may be sorry that you are mad at them, but they are not sorry they hit another child, and they will usually tell you so. Forcing them to apologize simply creates little hypocrites.

I have found that the best way to teach children manners is to model them. We need to display exquisite manners to children. When you interrupt a child who is in the middle of playing say, "Excuse me, I hate to interrupt you but. . . ." If I needed to speak to a teacher who was working with a child, I didn't walk up and begin talking to the teacher, acting as if the child didn't exist. I said to the child, "Excuse me, Sally, I need to talk to Martha," and I waited for Sally to nod or look up at me. That is so much more effective than lecturing to children.

Another technique that I have found very effective is to find a time when children are relaxed and not preoccupied, and slip a manners lesson in casually. One afternoon when my boys were about six and eight years old, I said very nonchalantly, "You know, adults are sometimes embarrassed around kids. They feel like they don't know what to say to kids. You can make them feel so much better about themselves if you put your hand out and shake theirs firmly and say, 'Hi, my name is Chris and I'm glad to meet you.' You can take away their fears."

It worked like a charm. They had never seen it that way. However, if I had approached them in a negative way, saying, "I noticed you were shy" or "You didn't say anything when my friend was here," I would have made them defensive and gotten a much less positive response.

A Very Few Basic Rules

Laying down the law on manners or making rigid rules about them is too burdensome for both children and adults, but that does not mean that we do not need to establish clear boundaries for children. I recommend that you settle on four, or at most five, basic rules which you are willing to consistently enforce. At CLC the rules are:

- people are not for hitting
- running is for outside
- put your work back when you are finished so that another child can use it
- juice and crackers stay in the juice and crackers area

These are very practical rules for running a classroom. You don't want ants all over the classroom so you don't allow children to wander around with food. Asking children to put their work back so another child can use it is a very pragmatic request that they can understand easily. "Running is for outside" gives children an appropriate picture in their minds. Words create pictures in children's minds and they act on those pictures. If you say, "don't run," the child sees a child running in his mind and in two minutes he's going to be running. If you say, "running is for outside," the picture changes to the appropriate environment. (Incidentally, adults are not so different from children in this regard. Think about the last time you were reading and felt hungry and thought "I'd like a dish of chocolate ice cream." I'd bet that within five minutes you were rummaging around in the freezer, looking for the ice cream. Once you create a picture in your mind, it's very hard to change.)

These are the kinds of rules you need to establish at home also. Parents should sit down with each other and decide on four or five rules that are unchangeable. Think about how you can present those rules so that they are clear, positive, and create the right pictures in the children's minds. After you've explained the rules, post them on the refrigerator as a reminder. Don't make up a new rule every day, but if you find that you do occasionally need to add one, make it a matter of family discussion. Children need to feel that expectations are not constantly changing, but that there is security. And you need to give them further security by being a disciplinarian. In many families today, the combined stresses of work and parenting make enforcing the rules seem too burdensome. But nothing is more terrifying to a child than parents who can't or won't set boundaries and enforce them. A chaotic spirit takes over in such children and they show little evidence of self-esteem.

However, the *way* we enforce the rules is almost as important as the fact that we enforce them.

Frequently, as a consultant traveling around the country, I observe teachers who seem to feel that they must assume an attitude of anger when they are about to discipline. That's unfortunate. At CLC, the children experience adults who are problem solvers and who are quietly (on the child's level) working with them to solve their interpersonal problems. The adults are not angry, but warm and clear in their directions, even to a child who is out of order.

Above all, adults assume that the child is in the right. The first attitude of the staff members is "how can I unravel this?" not "Johnnie's done it again." It's very important not to assume that the one who was in trouble before is the one who's in trouble now! If we understand that most discipline problems result from low self-esteem, it helps us avoid making bad assumptions. So, before beginning to mete out punishment or trying to change the child's behavior, the CLC staff considers the child's total life-picture, especially the at-home situation. If a child has a relaxed home and has a sense of well-being, there are no behavior problems because he is relaxed and happy when he comes to school. So why should we make it harder for the child who is having a tough time at home, by being "heavy" with discipline at school?

The Itemized Response

When the CLC's staff does have a persistent problem with a child, they may try a technique I borrowed from Synectics called the Itemized Response. The whole staff gathers in the afternoon in front of huge pads of paper and each of us simply writes down all the things that we appreciate about the child and his activities. Once we discover that the child is doing a number of exciting things, we may discover hidden treasures of activity and a lot that is likable about the "problem" child. Something may have been happening on the play-yard or in the art corner that simply wasn't appreciated by the entire staff so we create pages and pages of what we call "pluses" about the child. That way the staff enters the classroom the next day with a totally different attitude toward the child. All the adults are carrying in their hearts and minds the "good" things the child has been doing and thus are ready to verbally describe and credit the child for them.

I remember a black child named Jessie we had at the school several years ago. Jessie was really difficult. In fact, I got sick of hearing about all the things Jessie had done wrong. We had 60 children who were upper middle-class, but Jessie was from a decidedly disadvantaged home. He had no father, lots of brothers and sisters, and plenty of physical abuse in the family. I began to realize that everybody was down on him and was focusing his attention on what Jessie did wrong instead of the good things about him. So we declared an Itemized Response session for Jessie and we actually filled ten pages of honest, sincere, well-articulated pluses about Jessie, things that many of us had not known about him.

We were amazed at the things we appreciated about Jessie—his musical ability and his compassion, for example. In spite of all his negative behaviors, Jessie was very loving. If a boy or girl was hurt, he would be the first one to go comfort the child. His main problem was that he didn't have the built-in socialization skills or the modeling that middle-class children had.

We made a conscious decision not to talk to Jessie about his misbehaving, but to talk to him about his good behavior. Once we began focusing on his positive points, the whole spiritual environment of the classroom changed for Jessie and for us. We didn't come in expecting Jessie to be wrong. We came in delighted with all the things he did right. In that way, we turned around Jessie's behavior in one week. No one was complaining about his behavior because he had gotten the feedback that he was not in the wrong all the time.

When we did correct him, and we did, it was in another tone of voice. The change was so subtle that we didn't even realize it had happened at first. But when we saw the change it made in Jessie we said, "Let's do that for all the children we are concerned about." It changed the atmosphere in the whole classroom. Jessie taught us a lot.

The Itemized Response works well in families too. If you find the whole family is down on a particular child, the mother and father should sit down together and make a list of ten things they appreciate about the child. Then they should post it on the refrigerator so that the child can see that you could find ten good things about him or her.

This technique of writing down the pluses about children works wonders. Another "written-down" idea is this: If two children are squabbling, make them sit down while you write what each one says. If one child is feeling neglected—if you hear that familiar lament, "you treat Billy better than you treat me"—write down the complaint. Writing children's comments down seems to validate them. They feel that you really do understand what they've been saying, and once they feel you've heard them, they will stop whining and harping.

Whining is one behavior that annoys me terribly. When a child is whining, I write down all the whining words. Then I sit down calmly with the child and say, "Here's what you said, but you said it in such a whiny voice that it annoyed me and I couldn't hear what you were really saying. Now let's talk this through in a normal tone of voice and see if we can solve the problem so that you don't need to whine anymore." Children almost always respond positively to this approach.

This doesn't mean that we're going soft; it doesn't mean that we won't let the child know if he's off the mark. But, if we concede that most behavior results from low self-esteem, it seems the most exciting thing that we do is to use the Itemized Response to build self-esteem. And we do that by dwelling on the positive and by minimizing negative feedback. By our using that technique, children usually stop being problems and become exciting members of the classrooms.

The Discipline of Holding

If, however, the child is burdened too much and problems continue, I advocate holding as a disciplinary method. Simply holding a child on your lap for twenty minutes does a world of good. If you don't have the privilege of withdrawing with the child, hold him or her—firmly, but not too tightly—on your lap as you continue to teach.

It is particularly important to participate in the pursuit-and-struggle stage of holding. A child may kick and bite at first, but you must demonstrate your willingness to stick with him through the negative reactions until reconciliation occurs. Twenty minutes may elapse before the child relaxes, but afterward you will be that child's favorite teacher and vice versa. Nothing will work as fast as holding as a way of letting the child know that you really care about him and you're not going to *let* him misbehave.

I have found that children who have problems and who have built up a bad reputation with the other children and staff are changed by the holding technique. It reminds me of the story of the shepherd, and the sheep that kept continually straying. The shepherd broke one of the sheep's legs, placed the sheep around his shoulders, and carried it until the leg healed. By then, the sheep had become so much a part of the shepherd, he never wanted to stray.

At a CLC seminar several years ago, a woman shared a story with me that provides an excellent example of the effectiveness of holding. A mother was having problems with her thirteen-year-old daughter. The child wasn't in serious trouble, but she was exhibiting all the normal signs of adolescent rebellion, and communication between them was growing very strained. The mother heard about the holding technique at a church seminar and decided to try it. Every day when her daughter came home from school she insisted on holding her for twenty minutes.

At first, the daughter resisted, squirming and protesting, "Oh mother, this is stupid." But the mother persisted and things did become better between them. The daughter was less rebellious and their communication improved.

It had become so good that one day when the daughter came home and said, "I've had a horrible day, can't we forget holding for just one day?" the mother, not wanting to seem inflexible, agreed. However, several days later, in a quiet moment, the daughter said to her, "You remember that day when I was so upset and I asked if we could skip holding? That was the day when I really needed it most."

I see discipline as a part of the total tapestry of a program rather than an A-B-C formula. Everything that is done for children at CLC is aimed at increasing good discipline. The tone of voice the teachers use, the way they speak to children, the way the environment is set up, and the delineation of authority through the use of roles, all blend into this tapestry. For what a child really needs to know is that you respect him and trust him and love him. Children often know that we really love them, but they don't always know that we respect them.

These techniques have been used successfully for more than twenty years at CLC. We discovered that when you have teachers who lovingly expect children to follow through, an environment which is clearly thought out, and the teachers' roles clearly determined, classroom management and negative forms of discipline are almost eliminated. This frees both teachers and children to focus on their most important goal—the daily development of self-discipline. That, of course, is the ultimate goal of all discipline, whether at school or at home.

7

Recordkeeping

One of the most unusual and exciting things about the Children's Learning Center is its individualized approach to learning. Instead of a classroom of children who simultaneously learn by rote, it is a center for children who individually learn what each is ready to understand. And even more important, their self-esteem is not destroyed in the process of learning. There are no failures, nor are there "smart" children in the class. The self-defeating cycle of frustration at "failing" is eliminated.

This individualized learning process does have one major drawback, however. In an open classroom without a standardized curriculum, it is very difficult to keep accurate, up-to-date records of each child's progress. Montessori's solution to this problem was for teachers to keep "anecdotal" records, which involved writing at least one anecdote describing a child's work each day. In theory, this sounded good. In practice, it almost never happened. To be of any value, the anecdotes had to be at least a paragraph in length. That simply took too long for the average teacher working with five to seven students each day. Consequently, in the Montessori schools with which I'm familiar, daily records were seldom kept. Instead, about once a month everyone sat down and scrambled to get the records filled in, relying on admittedly hazy memories.

I struggled with this problem for several years, trying variations of the Montessori approach and others, but with little success. Finally, after borrowing a few techniques from the business world, I developed a remarkably accurate and remarkably simple system of recordkeeping that frees each teacher to tailor a child's curriculum.

When a child is enrolled in the Children's Learning Center a clipboard is created for him or her. On the clipboard is hung a sheet that lists in one column the days of the week, and in another column, across the top of the sheet, CLC's six instructional areas—language, math, sensorial, practical life, art, and music. (See chart below.) After the children leave each day, the teachers check off the areas in which each child has had a lesson. Then they decide if a child needs more time on a certain material or if he is ready to move on to a more complex task. With this system, at a quick glance a teacher can say, "Betty's had a lesson in music, language, and practical life this week. It's time for one in math."

In addition to these matrix sheets, each clipboard has a plastic bag with two 4 × 6 cards. On one card, the teachers describe what occurred in the lessons they had

TAKING CHILDREN SERIOUSLY

SUZY						
	Language	Math	Sensorial	Practical Life	Art	Music
MONDAY						
TUESDAY						
WEDNESDAY						
THURSDAY						
FRIDAY						

Week of _____ Oct. 4–8 _____

with the child that day. The notation must contain our "three pluses and a wish." The pluses have to be descriptive—"sounded out a word," "gave an example," etc. And they have to describe what went on in that one lesson; not for the whole day, but just that five- to ten-minute lesson.

The "wish" describes an area in which the child needs to improve or a way for him or her to grow in an understanding of a concept. For example, if I did a math lesson with Mary Lou, who was good at counting, but I didn't think she really understood multiplication, my wish might be to try multiplication with a different material the next time. Thus, the next teacher who had a math lesson with Mary Lou could look at my card and see the wish.

A list is also kept in the art area so that the art Rover can give check marks for all the art activities. If a child comes back and does some painting, and then works with clay or does some practical-life activities, not only is the in-depth lesson notated on the card, but these lessons in the art and practical-life area as well.

130

After he or she has filled out the format sheet and written the descriptive card, the teacher decides what lesson the child needs for the next day and, on the second card, writes a goal for that lesson. Every teacher has a pocket on the wall in the workroom and each child's goal cards that are assigned to a particular teacher are placed in that teacher's pocket at the end of the day. In that way, when the teachers come in the next morning all they have to do is pick up their cards and they are ready to start. This system insures that someone works with every child on a specific preplanned lesson every day. It also tells the staff what the children have accomplished and what they need to work on next.

To see how this system actually works, let's eavesdrop on a lesson that Brian is conducting with four-year-old Craig. They are working on a math lesson, using pebbles. Brian has drawn four circles. In the first circle he has placed four pebbles, in the second five, the third six, and in the fourth seven. He asks Craig to count the pebbles in each circle. After Craig has done so correctly twice, Brian encourages him to create his own counting circles. Craig then draws five circles and tells Brian the number of pebbles he will put in each. Brian encourages him to write the numeral for the number of pebbles in each circle and he does so, with a little help. Then he adds the correct number of pebbles and counts them several times.

The card that Brian writes about this lesson contains Craig's name, the subject, and the date at the top; below that are three descriptive statements and a "stretch." His three descriptive statements are: "was able to follow map directions," "set up his own counting circles," and "counted to nine several times on his own." The stretch or wish is, "to use the same format for division."

"I tried to write down what I saw, not what I thought or my opinion about our time together," Brian says. "I could have said, 'Craig really seemed to enjoy our time together,' or 'We had a really nice lesson.' That kind of evaluative language gives you some information, but not the kind of factual data I want to record about Craig."

Daily "Clipboard" Meetings

In addition to the more formal information contained on the cards, the staff shares informal information about the children at the daily clipboard meetings. At those meetings they write their cards, update their format sheets, and plan their goals for the next day.

At today's meeting Cathy shares an experience she has had today with Bradley. "I let him push me over and greatly exaggerated my movements as I fell," she says. "He loved it. He doesn't have a lot of physical strength, so I think it is important for him to have these opportunities to feel strong." Several other staff members chime in, agreeing. They note that Bradley frequently comes to school and refuses to answer to any name but "He-man." Leah speaks excitedly: "I have something great to share about Bradley. Today he told me, 'I'm not He-man anymore. Now I'm Bradley.'" Everyone is pleased with this growth in Bradley's acceptance of himself.

The teachers switch children every week, which keeps them from getting locked in. Constantly looking at each other's work forces a kind of community because the teachers are not going to write a poor card if they know another teacher will be reading it next week. This doesn't create competition among teachers. Instead, it fosters a loving kind of communication about each child. It promotes a real sense of teamwork.

The records system also helps teachers detect potential problems with children and deal with them in their early stages. When a child seems to stop learning, "shutting down" (because of a problem at home, perhaps) it doesn't take four weeks for the teacher to say to himself, "Gee, Sammy isn't doing as well as he did last month." It is evident immediately when Sammy loses interest and doesn't progress toward other learning materials. The staff can then plan to spend time observing Sammy, trying to identify his problem. In some cases, just recognizing the problem and letting the child know you know is sufficient to help him over the difficult time. It is not necessary to sacrifice several weeks before emotional distress is noticed.

A final advantage of the recordkeeping system is that it makes parent conferences much easier. Using the cards, the CLC staff can chart children's progress for their parents in several ways. They can look at the cards affectively, reading what each staff member has had to say about the child; or they can use them to give hard data on a child's achievements. For example, they can put all the language cards together and tell the parents, "Sharon has had twenty-five lessons in reading, she knows all her short vowels, and can read these five simple books."

I found this approach particularly effective with parents who were very concerned with their child's academic progress and who might have been a little concerned about our lack of a traditional curriculum—especially since most of our children became early readers and exhibited a good grasp of mathematical concepts.

Parents and Recordkeeping

The recordkeeping method easily can—and I think should—be adapted for use in the home. As a parent you can create clipboards and adopt your own categories; many parents won't choose to teach language, math, or sensorial activities to their children. However, you should not think "school" when you develop these matrix sheets. Think in a broader way.

I passionately believe that we need to develop a full tapestry of understanding for children, a full palette of colors. But that only happens with repeated interactions, not drillings, nor teachings, nor with workbooks. It takes place through thoughtful understanding on the part of parents who are aware that any moment with their children can be a learning moment. If you are sitting at your dining room table and you have put out the napkins which have a linen weave in them, you can talk about their interesting texture and how that kind of weaving is done. As you are riding in the car, point out the number and differing shades of green that you see in the trees ahead of you. You can sharpen the vision of a child by looking at a lake and saying, "Doesn't it look like it's full of diamonds today?" You can certainly enlarge the borders of your children's thinking by giving them a chance to see through your eyes the things that time, space, and experience have taught you.

The educational advantages of your home are enormous. Your "teaching" is really one-to-one tutoring, the most effective form of instruction. And as a parent, you get to practice that art from the moment your child is born. You are your child's most important educator, no matter where you eventually send him or her to school. The glue of helping children develop is what holds together the very fabric of your family life.

Always be on the lookout for opportunities to teach, and don't be afraid to try something new. If it doesn't work, give it up for now, but don't consider yourself or your child a failure if you try something one day and don't get feedback.

The young woman who does my hair has a three-year-old son. Recently, I made him a pull-a-word game. I covered a spaghetti box with colored paper and put cards in it on which I traced the letters of simple words, like cat and bat. On some cards I drew pictures and on others I cut them out from magazines. When I have my hair done I always spend a few minutes sounding out words with Skylar. I pull a card out and say, "this is 'kuh.' I'd like

You are important to me.

to hear your 'kuh.' This is 'aa.' I'd like to hear your 'aa.'"
He is a sweet little boy and he will always make the sound
but on some days it is obvious that he is not interested. He
is worried about the dog or distracted by something happening outside. When that happens, I just stop the game. I
never push him. But the next time I come, he'll almost
always come up to me and say, "k-a-t," as if he had been
storing it up and couldn't wait to share with me that he
could make those sounds.

In your home you can begin counting exercises with
your children by having them bring you three eggs or
four oranges from the refrigerator. If you ask for three
and they bring you four, say, "You're right, this many is
three and you've brought me one more which makes

four." Don't tell them that what they brought you is wrong, i.e., four when you asked for three. Credit them for the three and one more. Or if they bring you two and call it three, say, "that's part of three. This is two and add one to two and it makes three."

Your home tutoring provides immediate feedback and if you allow it, it will give you the ability to develop a learning strategy (or an architectural scheme) that will be tailor-made for your child.

However, in order for that to occur, you and your spouse need to sit down and decide what the most important aspects of being a human being are, and what character traits you want to develop in your children. For example, do you want your children to be honest, to be compassionate, to have a solid relationship with God? If so, it is not enough to hope they will absorb those values by osmosis. You and your spouse must plan how to inculcate these characteristics in them. The traits you choose will, of course, depend on your particular family background, its goals, wishes, and dreams. Once you have made your decisions, list those categories on your family clipboards. Then schedule regular meetings to review your records and discuss how well you are meeting your goals.

If one of your goals was to have your children develop a solid relationship with God, what have you done to encourage that? Do they see you praying or reading the Bible? Do you say grace at meals? Do you attend church regularly (not just drop them off at Sunday School)? Do you pray with them and talk about God as a normal part of your daily life?

Or, if you want your children to be forgiving persons, how forgiving have you been to them? When they miss the mark, are you ready to love, forgive, and help them or do you berate, put down, and shower them with anger? These are the kinds of questions you and your spouse need to ask yourselves in your meetings.

For parents, clipboards and cards can become a very loving form of communication about the children, especially if one parent works full time and the other stays home. The working parent is able to share in their children's first small achievements—their first steps, their first discoveries about their environment—as well as any problems that may be developing, without having to rely on the other parent's imperfect memory. Cards also make writing grandparents much easier. You can simply list the pluses on each child's card, without having to spend time creating a lengthy manuscript.

As you accumulate descriptive behavior about your children you will see patterns emerging. As they grow, you as parents can talk over these patterns and choose together to make the necessary changes as they arise. If you are careful to give fair descriptive feedback to children they will be able to see nuances in their behavior that are not clear to them when you simply yell, "Why don't you ever pay attention." Good managers don't give employees a task to do without giving them some parameters. We all need a road map to get started on a project or a journey. Unless children have some sense of the what, when, why not, and the how of behavior, they will not perform appropriately. I am reminded of the father who during a walk in the woods kept telling his nineteen-month-old son to "stay on the path" until the little boy finally said, "Daddy, what's a path?"

We need to help children see that their *behavior* and not *their results* is what really pleases us. Practice evaluating the quality of your children's behavior. Look at the how as well as the what in their performance. Start telling children what you like about the way they attained whatever small goal that you see they have achieved. "You were so gentle in the way that you handled the baby when you took that sharp object away from her." Don't focus on just the action itself, but start giving guidelines on innate skills that you see your children developing when they are still infants. Remember that love and trust will go a lot further toward changing a child than will anger and berating.

Bob Benson relates a wonderful story about the power of love to change a child's behavior in his book, *Come Share the Being:*

The rumors were that Mike was in some trouble. First they came from school and then of course they grew more rampant in the fertile soil of the church. And so we called a family council—Peg and I. "What are you going to do about it?" she said. "Well, what are you going to do about it?" was my reply. Will we confront him, will we ask him, will we assume that he didn't and treat him like he did? Will we accuse him, will we subtly tighten the reins of his freedom until he "cracks" and it becomes evident as to the truth of the rumors?

Now Peg is more of the "let's get this out in the open now" type and I . . . am generally willing to avoid, postpone, and run from all the confrontations, crisis and summit meetings that I possibly can. Unfortunately, this time she chose to defer to me as the leader of the home and turned the matter over to me.

"What are you going to do if it is not true?"

"I am going to continue to go into his room at night and kneel by his bed and I am going to rub his back for a moment and say, 'Mike I love you and I'm proud to be your dad. I hope you sleep well. I'll see you in the morning. Goodnight.'"

"And what are you going to do if it is true?"

"I am going to continue to go into his room at night and kneel by his bed and I am going to rub his back for a moment and say, 'Mike, I love you and I'm proud to be your dad. I hope you sleep well. I'll see you in the morning. Goodnight.'"

It was a couple of months later, he came first to his mom and then a week or so later to me and said, "I was in some trouble at school but I got it worked out. I'm sorry as I can be and it won't happen again."

I believe that love—steady, patient, unceasing, deep, expressed, oozed—is the only reliable option open to parents. It's better than advice, grounding, cutting the allowance, paddlings, punishments and threats or any other of the dozens of dodges and ruses we work on our unsuspecting and waiting children. Just care, just love, just show it.

Clipboards and cards help you show love by allowing you to spot skills you might otherwise overlook and to credit your children for them. Even letting the children know that you are keeping records honors them greatly. The children at CLC enjoyed the fact that we wrote cards about them. They often asked me if I had written down that they had done this or that.

Consistent, descriptive records might also provide another benefit to you as a parent. If one of your children develops a problem in school, you can share your cards with the child's teacher. While you may still need to take stronger action to modify the child's behavior, sharing with the teacher the concrete things your child does well may help to change the teacher's focus and give her "new glasses" with which to see the child.

In summary, whether they are used in the classroom or in the home, clipboards provide a sense of purpose and direction. They give the school staff, and ultimately the parents, a great deal of comfort. The information on the matrix sheet and the cards helps parents and teachers see the pattern of children's activities over weeks and months, and it also helps them provide a balanced diet of learning for each child every week.

8

Coaching

At the Children's Learning Center we created a unique program for staff development which we called coaching. Our coaching strategy grew out of our work with Synectics. George Prince, the founder of Synectics, believed that the staff of an organization needs constant, consistent feedback. We agreed. CLC coaching strategy works in tandem with the communication strategy. Through coaching, staff members put their communication skills into practice with each other.

CLC coaches are observers, noting and recording the activities of the rest of the staff. They perform an invaluable service. After editing their daily notes and the video, they give teachers in a session following school three positive points about their teaching and interaction with the children. The entire staff has the opportunity to see what a teacher is doing right. Also, each staff member is offered one wish to promote growth. Everyone learns from each other. This communication exchange makes coaching important to the CLC method of teaching.

Each day, after lunch, the staff assembles to review videotapes of their teaching, taken and edited by the Video Coach, and to hear the feedback from the Pad-and-Pencil Coach. The comments are all in the form of three pluses and a wish. The coaches are charged with describing three things that were positive for each person being reviewed, and giving the teacher being coached a wish for improvement or possible change in the lesson reviewed.

The pluses and the wish are worded in concrete phrases, not empty adjectives. A coach might say:

I like the way you bent over and smiled at Randy; I liked the way you held the rods when you presented them to him, so he could see their purpose; and I like the way you kept establishing eye contact with him. My wish is that you would have brought out the blue rods and put them together with the red rods to create a rectangle.

The Pad-and-Pencil Coach teaches in the morning, but the teachers filling that role also take pad and pencil with them and observe several other teachers, writing down things they want to coach them on. During the afternoon coaching session, they put these on big pads, mounted on an easel, and illustrate the wishes and pluses with pictures. The pictures make the feedback fun.

If the coach likes the way you were crediting a child, he

might draw a picture of a credit card. The second plus might be that you were really quiet, so he draws a quiet sign like in a hospital zone. If he feels you had good eye contact, he draws an eye. The wish might be that you ask fewer questions, but he won't write, "Don't ask questions." Instead, he'll draw a question mark with a slash through it.

Coaches use pictures because they have found that most people are so tuned in to what they do wrong, so self-critical, that if they write up three pluses and a wish in words, the person will never read the pluses. The teacher will zoom right over to the wish. The pictures are a visual aid. They force the teacher being coached to see that she did do a lot right and that there are good things she wants to continue doing.

The person being coached does not verbally respond. While this is initially difficult, ultimately, everyone appreciates not having to defend himself or herself. The feedback is offered in sincere appreciation and out of an honest desire to help. It does not require any defense. Each person accepts it in the attitude in which it is offered, friendly and supportive. Receiving a wish is like receiving a present. Everyone realizes that it takes some thought and effort for someone to find a growth point. Additionally, it is understood that the teacher may have satisfied the wish aspect after the coach stopped observing the event being coached; in which case, the teacher leaves the staff meeting with four pluses and the other staff members gain the benefit of the coach's perception.

Video Coach

After the pad-and-pencil coaching is finished, the Video Coach makes his presentation. The role of video person is a favorite, for it is fun and it allows the staff some creativity. The first thing in the morning the video person checks the list to see which staff members are to be video-coached that day. He also checks to see which children need to be filmed. Perhaps Julie has a parent conference coming up and no videotape is available of her work in art, or math, or some other subject.

Once he has the list of whom he needs to coach, the video person has complete freedom for three hours to be an artist. At the end of the morning, he plays the tape back, selecting thirty-second segments of each teacher to be coached, and noting the three pluses and a wish he wants to give each.

The Video Coach is given a whole day away from teaching to observe, to see for himself or herself what makes someone effective in teaching and what someone can do to be more effective. Literally, the coach's eyes are trained, through the eye of the camera, directly on the teaching. They are entirely focused on the positive aspects of teaching and the opportunities for growth. This focused concentration is perhaps one of the best "teachers" of all and a great secondary benefit of the video-coaching role.

At the afternoon staff meeting, the Video Coach plays back the coaching segments he has selected three times. The first showing gives the group an overview of the lesson. The second allows the group to write down the things that their co-worker was doing that are pluses in their minds. During the third showing, the group members ask that the tape be paused at action that needs a bit of positive feedback. Thus, the teachers being coached hear co-workers voice their appreciation for their work and everyone learns from each other. The Video Coach is the only one to offer a growth point or wish for the featured teacher. Again, there is no comment or defense given by the coached teacher.

Often when a teacher sees the tape he thinks, "Oh why was that piece selected? I look so clunky and I did so many other better things." But then he begins getting the feedback and says, "Gee, I didn't know I did that." He realizes that he has innate graces which he can make a conscious decision to use in the future. To see how well this system works, let's sit in on a video-coaching session.

Loren has been the Video Coach today and the staff is watching her taped segment of Sandra working with Jason. They are having a math lesson. Sandra holds out a basket filled with unifix cubes and asks Jason to take two out. When he does, she shows him a felt numeral 2 and traces it with his finger. Then she places the numeral on the floor and asks him to put the cubes next to it. When he has done several numbers this way she says enthusiastically, "I can tell you really know your numbers!" Jason nods his head solemnly as if to say, "of course, what did you expect?"

After watching it twice, staff members begin sharing the pluses with Sandra.

"Sandra, I really liked the fact that you kept emphasizing choice. You kept asking him to choose cubes from the basket so he knew that he was manipulating the materials," Frank says.

"Yes," Margaret chimes in, "you presented the cubes like a great gift for him to choose."

Jane says, "Sandra, I like the way you kept the pace of the lesson up. You kept him busy, kept him using his hands, so he had no chance to become bored. You showed great energy with him."

John adds: "Sandra, I was impressed by the way you credited him for knowing his numbers. You were so warm and encouraging that if I had been Jason I would have felt like a million dollars."

After a number of other pluses are given, it is time for Loren to share her wish for Sandra. "Sandra," she says, "I wish that you had had Jason count the lower-number cubes as he pulled them out of the basket. You did that when he got up into the higher numbers and he was having a little trouble, but I think he could have done it easily with the low numbers and that would have given him a feeling of success." Sandra thanks Loren for her wish and the video spotlight is turned on the next staff member.

When the coaching session ends, the Video Coach still has several tasks to complete. He must electronically transfer all the "choice" segments he has filmed that day to one of the tapes which are prepared and saved for parent conferences. CLC tries very hard to keep these tapes current. If any unused tape remains when this tape is completed, it is marked "Free" and stored for possible later use. As his last act of the day, the Video Coach covers the video, the camera lens, and the VTR cabinet, and makes sure everything is secure before he leaves.

Coaching, particularly video coaching, is not a new or an unusual technique. Universities and corporations use it all the time. But we found that video critiquing was usually a negative exercise which focuses on people's flaws. We discovered that students at the Children's Learning Institute were initially very anxious about being coached. Many of them had had painful experiences with it in other contexts. However, after one or two sessions, they looked forward to being coached; it's such a positive experience. We discovered that by the time new teachers had been on staff a week, they became very good at speaking differently and in using our materials, thanks largely to the positive feedback received through coaching and being able to comfortably learn from others' coaching. We learned that the CLC Institute could take almost any persons and turn them into excellent teachers in a few weeks using this process.

Coaching Is for Parents

Coaching is a way of respecting people, because you are willing to spend the time articulating the pluses as well as developing a wish. In that respect, it works just as well in families as in schools. From the time that their children are very small (eighteen months), till they are at least five or six, I think mothers and fathers should plan to coach each other on a regular basis, once a week, or once every two weeks. Caring enough to coach is a nice way for parents to honor each other.

If you are a father and you're watching your wife as she struggles to get the children dressed for Sunday School, grab an old envelope or whatever is handy and write down what she is doing at that moment, and the way she is doing it, that please you (after you offer to help, of course). Note the phrases she uses, her tone of voice, and the fact that she's not impatient, even though the clock is ticking. Jot down at least three positive things she's doing. Maybe you'll find that one thing she does is also driving you up the wall. Instead of letting that continue to irritate you, formulate a wish that you can share with her later.

On the other hand, if Mom is in the kitchen and Dad is out in the yard trying to get his yardwork done, and the children keep badgering him to answer questions or to help, she can jot down the things she appreciates about his way of interacting with them. Then she can add one wish that she thinks would help improve his communication. Formulating a wish can become a loving way of sharing with one's partner about a behavior one wishes would be changed. However, I want to give one word of caution. It's important not to give three pluses on the way the other person is communicating with the children and then se- lect as your wish that he or she would stop wearing the plaid shorts you hate so much. Pluses and wishes have to relate to one another. So, if your partner is doing some- thing that drives you crazy, sit down and make yourself think of pluses that relate to the wish. It may take a half hour and some hard thinking, but if you really think it through, it can be very effective.

To cite an obviously easy example, if your husband always leaves the cap off the toothpaste, you might first praise him for the way he hangs up the towels after he's through using them, the way he rinses out the sink when he's finished shaving, and the way he empties the bathroom trash basket without complaining. When you've complimented him on all those positive behaviors, he'll be much more receptive to your gentle reminder about the toothpaste cap.

Coaching is especially important for mothers who stay home all day with the children. The best gift a husband could give his wife would be his positive feedback on her mothering and teaching skills. He needs to find (or create) a quiet moment when they can relax, and then share with her his thoughtful observations.

Mothers who stay at home need that affirmation so badly. Men, and women who work, get some affirmation from their jobs. A woman who is at home with two preschool children doesn't get much at all.

The feedback should relate to her mothering skills, however, not the "great chicken dinner." To compliment her on her cooking is better than no affirmation at all, but she needs some feedback on her skills as a nurturing, loving parent. That's her job, in the same way that husbands' or working women's office work is their job. Office workers get regular, written performance reviews, as well as daily feedback from their supervisors and their co-workers. They can also judge how well they are doing by whether or not they got the "big account" or made the sale or won the case. With a child you may not know for twenty years if what you did today was right.

Coaching also works well with children and it is easy for parents to do. If you notice a child putting her doll or blocks away on the shelf, verbalize your appreciation right on the spot. "I really like the way you were putting the blocks back without anyone telling you to, and I like the way you put them back so neatly. You didn't just throw them back. And I like the way you were working so independently. You didn't need me for twenty minutes and it pleases me that you make those independent decisions to work just like Daddy does when he leaves for work in the morning." Your wish might be that she had looked across the room and noticed that this morning she had left Raggedy Andy off his home on the bed.

When you consider coaching in your family, remember that in the business world there are also "upward appraisal" schemes in which subordinates evaluate their superiors. In the same way, when children are allowed to evaluate their parents some fascinating insights can be shared. It's important not to laugh at your children's childish perceptions, but to solemnly write them down and take them seriously. Remember, "a little child shall lead them." Just the opportunity to try coaching their parents provides a tremendous growth experience for children.

I firmly believe that the kind of positive input that coaching gives is so powerful that if it were consistently applied, we could revolutionize our schools, our workplaces, and our homes.

Epilogue

In the beginning of this book, I said that one of my goals was to create education advocates for our children—to give parents insights into ways to improve their own interactions with their children and a yardstick by which to measure day-care facilities. I hope that I have achieved that goal. However, I realize that merely educating parents in what to look for in a child-care program does not guarantee they will be able to find it. CLC is unique and there is a tremendous scarcity of schools which offer any kind of quality care for young children. In the short run, parents may have to content themselves with applying these principles at home, while hoping that a national consensus about the importance of early childhood education develops *soon*.

As we have seen, the need for adequate child care has already reached near crisis proportions. As I write this, two child-care proposals, the Act for Better Childcare (ABC) and the Hatch Act, are slowly working their way through the United States Congress. ABC would provide $2.5 billion in funds for day-care centers, set minimum federal safety standards for day-care centers, and require care givers to update their training yearly. The Hatch Act would provide tax credits for corporations providing day care to their employees, provide $100 million to states to enable them to establish liability-insurance pools, $250 million to help businesses, educational institutions, and communities develop child-care facilities and $25 million in low-interest loans to day-care centers that need to expand. In addition to these government efforts, about three thousand of the nation's six million employers provide some sort of child-care assistance, but most merely provide advice or referrals. In some communities, school boards are expanding their preschool programs and churches are expanding their day-care facilities or adding new ones. All of these efforts are admirable and necessary. To solve a problem of this magnitude will require the best efforts of all sectors of our society.

However, I believe there is another potential answer to this problem that is being overlooked, or at best, downplayed, and that is involvement of mothers themselves. Although millions of women have found fulfillment in careers and would no more consider giving them up to return to the role of full-time homemakers than would most men, not every woman wants to put on a business suit and go off to the office each day. In fact, in spite of the inroads women have made into many professions, most of them still work in traditional "pink ghetto" jobs, where the pay is low and the stress is high.

Although I believe that many women still entertain the old-fashioned idea that full-time mothering can be a calling, not a chore, few women today, married or single, can afford the luxury of not working. However, if women could see that it can be a challenging career to stay home and take care of children, and if they could make money doing it, I believe many of them would choose to do that. I see no reason why a woman who stays home and takes care of five children shouldn't be paid as much as the average executive secretary, for example. At least one of the 1988 presidential candidates has recognized the potential of this option and has proposed providing tax credits for family day-care centers. Family day care is certainly not a panacea, but we cannot afford to neglect any potential weapon of our arsenal in our attack on this problem.

I have thought a great deal about this since I left CLC and I am convinced that the principles I have described in this book could be used to train women to provide quality home child care for infants through preschoolers. Even the best school cannot duplicate the loving environment of a home; I believe that properly trained women could provide the best of both worlds for children—a caring family environment and an excellent education. It is my dream to help inaugurate such a program. But that is another story.

APPENDIX

The Children's Learning Center Materials Sources

General Learning Materials

J. A. Preston Corporation (equipment for special children)
60 Page Road
Clifton, NJ 07012
(800) 631-7277

Brio Corp (beautiful wooden building materials)
6531 North Sidney Place
Milwaukee, WI 53209
(414) 352-5790

Cuisenaire Co. (unifix, cuisenaire, chip trading, pattern
  blocks)
12 Church Street, Box D
New Rochelle, NY 10802
(800) 237-3142

Didax, Inc. (unifix materials)
Educational Resources
5 Fourth Street–Centennial Industrial Park
Peabody, MA 01960
(617) 535–4757/87

English Garden Toys (trampoline, hoops)
Medrad Drive
Route 910
Indianola, PA 15051
(800) 445–5675

ETA–Mathematics Catalog
199 Carpenter Avenue
Wheeling, IL 60090
(800) 445–5985

Fun-damentals (problem-solving cards)
42 Boston Post Road
Guilford, CT 96437
(203) 453-6525

Music Resources International
P.O. Box 195
Walton, NY 13856
(607) 865-7939

Lego Systems, Inc.
555 Taylor Street
Enfield, CT 06082
(203) 749-2291

Olive Branch Developmental Toys (Runk-A-Dunka)
Sorrento, ME 04677
(207) 422–6755

Puppet Productions, Inc. (beautiful puppets—Elsie, etc.)
P.O. Box 82008
San Diego, CA 92138
(800) 854–2151

Step, Inc. (Stepboard materials)
P.O. Box 887
Mukilteo, WA 98275
(800) 225-STEP

Taskmaster Ltd.
Morris Road Clarendon Park
Leicester, LE2 6BR
England
Phone: 704286

Montessori Materials

American Montessori Society
150 Fifth Avenue
New York, NY 10011
(212) 924-3209

Kantoor, fabrieken en toonzalen
Industriepark 14
P.O. Box 16
7021 BL Zelhem
Holland
Phone: (0)8342-1841

Montessori Services
(Montessori Practical Life supplies—pitchers, spoons,
trays, etc.)
228 South "A" Street
Santa Rosa, CA 95401
(707) 579-3003

Nienhuis Montessori U.S.A. (classic Montessori materials)
320 Pioneer Way
Mountain View, CA 94041
(415) 964-2735

Toys for Life (beautiful variations on classic Montessori
materials)
320 Pioneer Way
Mountain View, CA 94041
(415) 964-2735

Materials for Infants

Weimer-Ferguson Child Products
P.O. Box 10427
Denver, CO 80210
(303) 733–0848

Science Materials

Teacher's Laboratory, Inc.
P.O. Box 6480
Brattleboro, VT 05301
(802) 254–3457

Art Materials

Brittoys (GALT materials)
Attention: U.S. Sales & Inquiries
3111 Broadway
New York, NY 10027
(212) 865–1626

Hammet (pencils)
2393 Vauxhall Road
Union, NJ 07083
(800) 526–4518

Materials for Older Children

The Nature Company
P.O. Box 2310
Berkeley, CA 94702
(800) 227–1114

Wide World Games (age 10 and up)
Colchester, CT 06415
(203) 537–2325

Computer Software

Hammet
44 West Ferris Street
East Brunswick, NJ 08016
(800) 225–5467

Learning Company
P.O. Box 2168
Menlo, CA 94026
(800) 525-2255

Music Systems for Learning, Inc.
311 East 38th Street
Suite 20 C
New York, NY 10016
(212) 661-6096

Trampoline and Outdoor Equipment Resources

Sidlinger Trampoline
901 West Miller
Garland, TX 75041
(800) 322-2211

Little River Industries, Inc.
P.O. Box 505
Quincy, FL 32351
(904) 875-2300

Miracle Recreation Equipment Co.
P.O. Box 420
Monett, MO 65708
(417) 235-6917

Note: We had a thick foam mat custom made to border the trampoline. An upholsterer made a heavy-duty cover for the mat. DaSilva Upholstery, 11 Elmar Drive, Danbury, CT 06810.

Other

Gesell Materials
Program for Education, Inc., Dept. W84
Box 167
Rosemont, NJ 08556
(609) 397-2214